There are many books on change management that provide Do's and Don'ts and advice, but this book provides practical tools that the LEGO Group has developed and honed to get people to be actively part of the change. These interventions, mostly for workshops, are laid out in train the trainer fashion with detailed guidance on preparation, facilitation and followup. Thanks to the LEGO Group for sharing what you have learned internally!

Jeffrey K. Liker, Professor Emeritus,
University of Michigan and Shingo Prize winning author of The Toyota Way

In *Leading Transformations*, author Gitte Jakobson delivers an insightful and invaluable guide on navigating the complex world of managing and leading transformation at one of the most iconic companies in the world: The LEGO Group. Drawing on behavioural science as the foundations to drive successful change, this book delves into the people side of change and how to adopt practical approaches that enable understanding, predicting and influencing of human behaviour. *Leading Transformations* provides a compelling framework with real-life examples, tools and strategies needed to manage and lead change effectively. Whether you're a people manager, change practitioner or business leader looking to make a lasting impact, this book will provide you with invaluable insights to develop your own leadership capabilities and accelerate your impact in leading change.

Melanie Warner, Head of Solutions EMEA, MindGym

Many books have been written on this subject. What makes this book stand out from others is that Gitte has, and is still, living and breathing transformation in her everyday work. As in her previous book, Gitte has the unique ability to combine practice with reflection in a very down-to-earth style that is refreshing. Definitely a great handbook for anyone looking for guidance through a change process in the workplace.

Stephen Joseph Burke, Organizational Psychologist Coach,
Co-Owner Burke & Marcussen

Building an organization capable of change and transformation, as well as creating capacity and ability for change, is a task only a person of Gitte Jakobsen's talent and experience could lead. In this important and practical book, she explains the journey she took helping guide The LEGO Group to restore profitability and prepare for future growth in new and existing markets. More specifically, Jakobsen tells us just how she led the process and the ways it transformed one of the best companies on the planet.

Patrick Graupp, Vice President & Senior Master Trainer, TWI Institute

Leading Transformations

The world and its business environments are in a state of constant change. The reality today is that organizations and their leaders are faced with increasingly daunting demands for change and, unless they build organizations that can keep pace with these fast-changing environments, it will be a challenge simply to survive while, at the same time, continuing to thrive and embrace uncertainty and disorder.

One effective example of a world-renowned company that survived an existential crisis to become one of the most iconic companies in the World: The LEGO Group. In *Building a Global Learning Organization* (CRC Press, 2014), the authors showed how to develop and implement a global structure for learning based on the TWI (Training Within Industry) methods of good supervision. The goal was to create and sustain standardized work across multiple languages and cultural platforms to maintain the highest quality of the product as the company expanded internationally. In that book, you learn how the LEGO Group, as a multinational global company, worked on business transformation through changes in organizational learning systems, including new ways of working and other Lean transformational initiatives. Great organizations across the globe have used this text as a benchmark for global and national rollouts of TWI programs and standard work initiatives.

Based on this rich experience of building a global learning organization, it became clear that basic structures needed to be put into place in order to effectively create and manage the change process.

In this book, you get inspiration on how the LEGO Group met these challenges by developing and implementing a framework for transformations to create a common approach to designing, leading and anchoring change in an effective and impactful way. The author gives you *insights* into the journey which began by designing the LEGO Way of Change. She describes the process of testing the approach in a bigger transformation which, based on pilot learnings, was implemented in transformational initiatives. This book outlines some of the approaches that the LEGO Group implemented in order to ensure change would be both successfully implemented and sustained, including in-depth guides on impactful interventions with both leaders and people in the organization.

The author discusses personalizing and navigating change as well as designing change in the organization and measuring its impact. You will continue learning more from specific real-life case studies from business leaders focused on different kinds of transformation, from reshaping functional teams to optimizing lead time through improved ways of working.

When it comes down to it, change is about the people side of the equation. It is easy to change strategy, process, or technology, but it is harder to change individuals, people, and their behaviors. This book will provide inspiration and guidance on how to bring the people side of change into play in an effective and impactful way.

Leading Transformations

Using the LEGO® Way of Change to Drive Transformations Effectively and Successfully

Gitte Jakobsen

Foreword by Patrick Graupp

Routledge
Taylor & Francis Group

A PRODUCTIVITY PRESS BOOK

First published 2024
by Routledge
605 Third Avenue, New York, NY 10158

and by Routledge
4 Park Square, Milton Park, Abingdon, Oxon, OX14 4RN
Routledge is an imprint of the Taylor & Francis Group, an informa business

ISBN: 9781032152226 (hbk)
ISBN: 9781032152219 (pbk)
ISBN: 9781003243113 (ebk)

DOI: 10.4324/9781003243113

Typeset in Cera Pro
by Deanta Global Publishing Services, Chennai, India

My family lived through yet another book – thanks for your love and support: Peter, Sarah, and Julie. Thanks for your patience and sacrifices through evenings, weekends, and vacations while I worked on the book.

I would like to dedicate this book to my parents Birthe and Erik with love. Thanks for setting me on the road fully equipped with curiosity and courage – thanks for always believing in me and for your unconditional support of my ideas and dreams.

CONTENTS

FOREWORD

As a young boy of five or six years old living on an Air Force base in Germany with three brothers, I remember vividly the night my father brought home what was to me at that age a huge box with a picture on the top of children building houses out of plastic bricks. The set included toy cars and a fold-out platform printed with streets and green yards to put the houses on in a pretend town that we played with for hours on end. The plastic bricks, square and rectangle, only came in two colors, white and red, but included little windows and doors. For some reason, I loved those windows and eagerly built the houses around them. It was 1963 or 1964.

Fast forward a decade and a half and my brothers and I were all heading for engineering careers, though I switched my major at Drexel University at the end of my freshman year to Humanities and Communication as I headed off to Japan for six months to work in my Japanese mother's cousin's backyard plastic injection molding factory. The year was 1977 and the world was just starting to take notice of Japan's industrial rise. My mother and her family had grown up during World War II and I was going there to search for my roots. That was the start of my life-long love of language, culture, food, and (surprisingly) a program called Training Within Industry, or TWI.

I went back to Japan as soon as I graduated from Drexel having studied Japanese at the nearby University of Pennsylvania. I had the very good fortune of immediately finding a job with Sanyo Electric Co. where I began teaching English to Japanese staff being assigned overseas to factories and sales offices as Japanese companies rapidly expanded all over the world in the 1980s. The man who hired me at Sanyo's brand-new Training Center in Kobe, Mr. Kazuhiko Shibuya, told me on my first day on the job, "Pat, you have a lot to learn. But first TWI." Mr. Shibuya saw me as much more than a mere English teacher and I am forever grateful.

I left Sanyo after a 20-year career that also took me on a 5-year stint to a new compact disc manufacturing plant in Indiana, back to Japan to lead Sanyo's overseas training development, and finally to San Diego where I led Human Resources for the North American region, including five large plants in nearby Tijuana, Mexico. The week after 9–11, I was planning to take some vacation time to introduce TWI to some interested people in Syracuse, NY, and they told me, "If you make it, great. If you can't make it, everyone will understand." I made it and was on one of the first flights that took off after the attack. Interest in TWI was still small but enough to convince me to leave Sanyo and work exclusively on reintroducing the program back to the country of its birth, the USA, where it was developed during World War II.

The Department of War knew very early in that conflict that, while the fighting would take place in Europe and Asia, production for the war effort would have to happen in the USA. But all the experienced workers in shipyards and factories across the country were heading off to fight leaving behind an inexperienced workforce consisting of, for the first time, women going into a manufacturing environment. This was the era of Rosie the Riveter. Our leaders knew that Rosie could not be treated the same way as the men who came before her when they were introduced into the rough and tumble environment of a factory or shipyard but, if they failed, we would surely lose the war. The answer to this challenge was the incredibly successful TWI training program. It was so successful that after the war it was shared around the world, most notably in Japan where it became a foundation for the country's industrial resurgence.

Working out of his Syracuse office, Bob Wrona, the person who contacted me about piloting the TWI courses, and I began running TWI classes for small and medium-size companies in New York, North Dakota, Minnesota, and Texas. Before long, a few major companies began finding TWI on their own and reached out to us to help them put on classes. A plant manager at McCormick Spice, who had just come from Pepsi Cola, told me when I met him in Baltimore that he had been struggling with his Lean implementation there and discovered the TWI program late in the night as he searched the internet for solutions. Not surprisingly, large auto parts manufacturers also called us after they were told by Toyota to get TWI. It was not long after that the Toyota Way series of books began appearing that described Toyota's use of TWI and how it was a central component of the vaunted Toyota Production System, the foundation of the Lean manufacturing movement.

One day toward the end of 2009, Bob called me and told me about his conversation with a person from LEGO in Denmark who was putting together a program that sought to standardize the work of the LEGO plants in different countries – Denmark, the home country, Hungary, Czech Republic, and their newest plant in Mexico. The key to the success of the LEGO product, she explained, was the "clutch power" of thousands of unique plastic parts that all had to fit snugly together with one another regardless of where any individual piece was manufactured. They had just completed a year of preparation and had decided on the core skills program they would use for the effort – TWI Job Instruction.

That person was Gitte Jakobsen and we wrote about these experiences in our book, *Building a Global Learning Organization: Using TWI to Succeed with Strategic Workforce Expansion in the LEGO Group*.

At first, Gitte asked Bob to just give her the training manuals and they would take it from there because, after all, she and her colleagues were experienced trainers and Gitte herself was an organizational development expert. Bob said no. The TWI programs were uniquely developed, he explained to her, and they could not be put on properly and effectively without actual plant-side implementation and practice with an experienced TWI expert. Gitte was taken aback at first and, perhaps, a bit humiliated (Bob had a way of doing that with people). But later she professed in public her gratitude for Bob's insistence, and his stubbornness, in taking them down the right path to success with TWI. This proved itself to be true when LEGO opened yet another huge plant in China and put to use its newfound TWI skills to effectively start production there efficiently and on time.

That's how I met Gitte and we worked together closely for several years introducing and anchoring TWI Job Instruction and Job Relations throughout the LEGO family of manufacturing plants. On one of my many visits to Billund, Denmark, the home of The LEGO Group, she took me to the LEGO House where employees meet and work in an inspiring environment designed to bring out creativity and joy. Visitors to the house also go through a room filled with wide white drawers and are asked, "What year were you born?" In the room, I answered 1958 and the host opened up the appropriate drawer and took out a pristine LEGO set from that era that would have been played with by me as a child. Gitte told me that it was not unusual at that moment for people to break down in tears seeing the prized toy of their childhood and I confess I was also close to that point.

After her success creating, building, and leading the Learning Center at the LEGO Group, Gitte went on to a new and important assignment leading leadership development that could build an organization capable of change and transformation. This was imperative as the company headed into its next existential challenge to restoring profitability and preparing for future growth in new and existing markets. In this book, Gitte explains the journey the LEGO Group took in creating capacity and ability for change and, more specifically, tells us just how they did it. There is no person better qualified to teach us how to do this than Gitte with her deep background and experience leading people in one of the best companies on the planet.

Reviewing the journey the LEGO Group has taken over close to one hundred years, I'm reflecting personally on how my brothers and I were influenced by those red and white plastic bricks, and the young child I was, fitting the windows into the spaces and building the toy houses around them. The mission of the LEGO Group is to "inspire and develop the builders of tomorrow"; they have been performing that role relentlessly as much more than a mere toy company. With inspiring people like Gitte at the helm, I'm confident that the LEGO Group will continue to grow and prosper based on this promise and I've been honored and privileged to have played a small part in that history.

Patrick Graupp
Owner, Vice President, and Senior Master Trainer
The TWI Institute

ACKNOWLEDGMENTS

I have been incredibly fortunate to work with a group of talented and passionate people in the LEGO Group and would like to express my appreciation for the commitment they have shown to the LEGO Way of Change initiative, both through development and execution of this approach and, additionally, through their contributions to the completion of this book.

First of all, I would like to thank Jakob Meiling for his endless support throughout the process, and for removing roadblocks and providing strong guidance in the process of realization of this book and making my dream come true. And, additionally, a big thank you to Knud Hougaard, Thomas Sørensen, and Patrick van den Akker for their support on the legal and graphical parts.

My dear colleagues from the Change and Transformation Team: Ida Vinther, Paul Jarowicki, Anne Rønne, Eva Vig, Pallavi Kumar, and Stine Jespersen – thanks for your relentless energy in our collaboration in the LEGO Way of Change, and for being amazing Change Rock Stars.

There is no better assembly of enlightened leadership than can be found in the LEGO Group who contributed with their personal leadership stories to make the book real and relatable to the leadership context. I would like to thank and share my admiration for the following business leaders: Torsten Bjørn, Palle Ditlevsen, Kasper Thams, Helle Liltorp Johnson, Jan Juul Severinsen, and Annette Rosendahl.

I am also very thankful to the great people outside of the LEGO Group who have supported my journey.

I would like to express my sincerest gratitude to MindGym. It was a great experience to co-create and develop the LEGO Way of Change together with you based on your strong domain expertise and experience and making it fit into the culture of the LEGO Group. As well, I would like to express my genuine appreciation to MindGym and their dedicated staff for granting me a non-exclusive license to include MindGym materials in Chapters 3–8 of the book. This is a significant contribution, and thanks for your guidance and review of the manuscript to retain the integrity of the fantastic and impactful MindGym approach.

Finally, I would like to thank Patrick Graupp who believed in and supported this project wholeheartedly from day one. Thanks for guiding and coaching me and for taking on the huge task of editing this book. Without you, I would never have reached this achievement.

ABOUT THE AUTHOR

 **Gitte Jakobsen** has been involved in organizational and business development for learning and transformations in the LEGO Group since 1997. She has held roles as staff manager and project director in the LEGO marketing arena as well as Human Resources. Over the last five years she has acted as transformation director for the Strategy and Transformation team leading and facilitating strategic transformations. She has extensive experience in the development and execution of strategic learning and transformational initiatives across the product development, marketing, operations, and commercial business areas and spanning multiple cultures.

Jakobsen holds a Master's degree in educational psychology from the University of Aarhus, Denmark. With a deep and holistic practical experience and theoretical foundation, she implemented a Global Job Training Organization across manufacturing sites in multiple countries for the LEGO Group. She shared the results and the learnings of this process together with Patrick Graupp and John Vellema in their book, *Building a Global Learning Organization*, which received a Shingo Publication Award in 2015.

CHAPTER 1

INTRODUCTION
The LEGO® Group and Its Transformations

In 2017, the LEGO Brand was named the most powerful brand in the world. The LEGO Group is built on a foundation of strong brand appeal as LEGO products and experiences have spanned generations of children at play. This success is based on strong LEGO values considering play as essential to how children learn and that meaningful play experiences help shape children in a profoundly positive way for the rest of their lives.[1] In 2022, the LEGO Group celebrated its 90th anniversary – and the year 2032 will be a seminal event in history. It will be the year the LEGO brand turns 100 years old. The LEGO brand has been one of the most popular toy brands in the world for decades, and over these decades, the company has grown steadily. But the company has also faced problems along the way, and there have naturally been ups and downs. This becomes clear when we look back on the LEGO history and the transformations that have made the company what it is today. The objective of this introduction is to give a brief insight into the transformations in LEGO Group, which clearly created the need for developing a LEGO approach on how to manage and lead transformations.

How It All Started – Setting Up Business and Early Struggles

In 1916, at the age of 24, Ole Kirk Kristiansen bought the Billund Joinery in Denmark – a woodworking factory that made doors, windows, kitchen cabinets, cupboards, coffins, chests of drawers, and tools for digging peat. All of its work was of first-class quality, which was important to him. Gradually the business broadened its scope and tackled bigger projects.

The business, however, was ravaged by several fires throughout its history. The first occurred in 1924 when his sons, Godtfred and Karl Georg, were playing in the workshop while Ole Kirk Kristiansen and his wife Kristine were taking a midday

DOI: 10.4324/9781003243113-1

nap. The boys found a box of matches on a workbench and tried lighting the glue heater for a bit of warmth. The fire spread to some wood shavings and the factory as well as the house burnt to the ground. Godtfred, who would take over the company from his father, later said, "My first achievement was to burn down the workshop and house."

Ole Kirk Kristiansen was very fond of children. From scraps of waste wood in his workshop, he would skillfully make miniature versions of various full-size products he was making in the factory and give them to children, so the jump to wooden toys was not a big one. There is no denying his craftsman's eye for detail – the finely sanded corners, smooth wood finishes, and many coats of varnish. His hobby would soon become his life work.

The Beginning of the LEGO Group

The global depression and economic crisis of the time forced Ole Kirk Kristiansen and his carpentry business to produce new and easy-to-sell products which marked the beginning of the LEGO Group as it started to make wooden toys, such as cars, airplanes, and yo-yos. It was a tough beginning for the company and he had to reach out to his family for help. But they did not always agree with him. When he asked his brothers and sisters to act as guarantors for a loan to secure the company's future, one of them asked, "Can't you find something more useful to do?"[2] Ole Kirk Kristiansen repaid the loan with interest in 1939 and, as his son Godtfred later recalled, "It was a big day in his life."

Until 1934, the business manufactured buildings, furniture, and toys, but that was the year he decided to concentrate on toy production. This decision involved finding a new name for the company and Ole Kirk Kristiansen decided to hold a competition among his employees to find a good name for the business with the prize being a bottle of his home-made wine. The competition winner was... (wait for it!) Ole Kirk Kristiansen himself. He played with the two Danish words LEG and GODT (meaning Play Well) to come up with the name LEGO. The intention of the name was to reflect the quality and children's right to enjoy play.

Within a few years, Ole Kirk Kristiansen had laid the foundations of what was to become one of the world's leading toy making companies.

Quality Above All

Ole Kirk Kristiansen always guaranteed the quality of his work, something he continued to do in his work with wooden toys. He was convinced that children deserved toys of high quality, made of the finest materials so that they would last for many years of play. He only used beechwood which was first air-dried for two years and then kiln-dried for three weeks. It was then cut, sanded, polished, and given three coats of varnish or paint, just like real furniture. Quality was demanded at every stage of the process, especially from his own children. Godtfred once took a consignment of painted wooden ducks to the railway station for sale. Back at the factory, he proudly told his father how he had done something really clever and saved the company money. "How did you manage that?" asked Ole Kirk

Kristiansen. "I gave the ducks just two coats of varnish, not three as we usually do!" said his son proudly. His father's prompt and stern response flew back in his face:

> You'll immediately fetch those ducks back, give them the last coat of varnish, pack them and return them to the station! *And* you'll do it on your own – even if it takes you all night!

"That taught me a lesson about quality," said Godtfred Kirk Kristiansen on a later occasion.[3] After the lesson, Godtfred Kirk Kristiansen carved wooden signs with the company motto, "Only the Best Is Good Enough" and hung them on the walls of the factory to remind employees of the company's attitude to quality.

Ole Kirk Kristiansen was interested in all forms of new technology which could improve quality and rationalize production. His interest in new technology, new tools and machinery, and new materials and processing methods was obvious when it came to running his own company. He had the gift of spotting potential, an ability his immediate family occasionally viewed with some skepticism. He bought his first milling machine in Germany in the mid-1930s. There was no doubt he was making a significant financial investment. The sum he paid for the machine equaled one-third of the company's total profit for the previous year. Irrespective of the price of the milling machine, Ole Kirk Kristiansen had no doubt about the investment – the machine would increase the quality of the wooden toys.

Children Need Toys – Even in Hard Times

The outbreak of World War II did nothing to limit toy production. In times of crisis, the demand for toys was greater than ever. During the first two years of the war, the company doubled its sales. Due to the war, all import activity was halted which naturally favored the sale of Danish-made goods. Later, it was forbidden to use metal and rubber for nonessential goods, like toys. All of these factors boosted the production of Danish wooden toys and thus also the LEGO production.

As noted earlier, the business was ravaged by fire several times throughout its history and a major fire in 1942 burned Ole Kirk Kristiansen's life achievement to the ground, almost destroying in the process his will to carry on. Only his sense of responsibility for his sons and employees persuaded him to rebuild the factory and carry on even as the insurance on the business would not cover the loss and reconstruction.

With the assistance and support of family and employees a new factory was built on the site of the old workshop. The new factory was more modern than its old counterpart and better suited for the mass production of toys which meant a rise in productivity from 1943 onward.

Experimenting with Plastics

By the end of World War II, Ole Kirk Kristiansen was finding it increasingly difficult to source beechwood of the right quality. At the same time, the post-war period presented industry with new options in modern plastics and technology. He decided to commit to the new trend and invest in an expensive plastic injection molding machine. In 1946, Ole Kirk Kristiansen and other Danish toy manufacturers attended a demonstration of an injection molding machine. He was enthusiastic about the technology and placed an order for the machine. The British molding machine arrived in Billund in late 1947. Molding tools and raw materials were difficult to come by and much experimentation was necessary in order to gain experience in the molding process.

The new injection molding machine was installed in a building next to the woodworking factory after it had been tested in the basement of Godtfred Kirk Christiansen's home. While still getting acquainted with plastic molding, the company introduced its first plastic products in 1948. However, it was not until 1949 that plastic production really started heating up.

In the late 1940s, Ole Kirk Kristiansen and his son Godtfred were presented with plastic cubes from a British manufacturer, a novel idea they were promoting. The LEGO team began redesigning the cubes so they could be better assembled and, in 1949, the company launched its first building set: Automatic Binding Bricks.

The "LEGO Brick" and Expansion Abroad

In 1951, the name Automatic Binding Bricks was supplemented with the Danish name LEGO Mursten (literally, LEGO bricks) because Godtfred Kirk Christiansen, who by this time was assuming more and more responsibility running the company up through the 1950s, wanted to establish wider recognition of the LEGO name. He contemplated how the toy market could develop once post-war import restrictions on competitor products were lifted and what this could mean for exports of LEGO products as well. He began to look beyond the Danish market and the first step on the way to becoming a global enterprise was taken in Norway. Attention turned then to Germany, the global center of toy production. Godtfred Kirk Kristiansen claimed, "If we can conquer Germany, we can conquer the whole world!"

Focus on Product Development

With the LEGO® system now well established, the market was ready for product differentiation. This meant a need for more focus on product development and a special product development department, LEGO Futura, which was set up in Billund in 1965. Its employees were to concentrate on developing the product and testing their ideas together with children.

The LEGO Group went through a lot of transformations during the 1970s, including the introduction of an even stronger focus on product safety, the creation of a completely new organization in the US, and the establishment of a new production facility outside Denmark. This was all a part of navigating an ever-changing business landscape.

Stagnation

Following decades of growth and great efforts at transforming the company into a modern, international presence, sales started to slow down in the early 1970s, putting the company in unfamiliar waters. At the same time, management was having internal discussions on whether the LEGO brick should be viewed as a toy or, perhaps, something more. This resulted in third-generation owner Kjeld Kirk Kristiansen, grandson of the founder Ole Kirk Kristiansen, introducing his thoughts and ideas on the company's future direction in 1978. To Kjeld Kirk Kristiansen, the LEGO brick was not just a toy – it was both play and learning material possessing endless possibilities. His new mindset injected fresh energy into the company from the late 1970s onwards.

The LEGO Group had been blessed with growth, progress, and increased production since the 1950s. However, the world was changing. The 1973 oil crisis temporarily slowed market expansion and, in the face of sluggish sales results, particularly in the American market, the LEGO Group experienced its first bout of stagnation – one effect of which was unsold retail inventories and an oversupply of molding capacity. The company decided to mothball 101 new molding machines. The workforce was also reduced drastically to trim the organization to the new reality. Between 1974 and 1977, the number of employees was reduced from 2097 to 1162.

The Next Generation

After a long period with two self-taught enthusiasts at the head of the company, Ole Kirk Kristiansen and his son Godtfred, a new era was calling for more professional corporate management. Kjeld Kirk Kristiansen was appointed Chief Executive Officer in 1979.

Kjeld Kirk Kristiansen was studying at IMD, the International Institute for Management Development in Lausanne, Switzerland. He returned to Denmark in 1977 to join the LEGO Group management. Although much of this time was spent in Switzerland, he also spent a part of his time in the US, helping with the establishment of a new US sales organization. Returning to Denmark, Kjeld Kirk Kristiansen brought many new ideas with him from his time at IMD and one of his first steps was to introduce a brand new product development model to be known as "System within a system." With this fresh approach, the company was able to navigate through the remainder of the century.

After nearly 20 years at the helm, in 1998, Kjeld Kirk Kristiansen appointed Poul Plougmann as chief financial officer and, a year later, handed over day-to-day management of the company to his management team in order to turn the LEGO Group around and return it to profitability once again. This was accomplished by trimming the organization through what was called the Fitness Plan. In the short term, cutting the company's costs was successful, but at the same time, continuity and profitability was not realized as expected.

Crisis

Poor results require changes in senior management, and the same was true at the LEGO Group. After a long period of bouncing between losses and profit, the

2003 fiscal year ended with yet another deficit – this time in the amount of billions of Danish Kroner. Following this massive loss, Kjeld Kirk Kristiansen once again resumed the reins of day-to-day management and spent the next 10 months charting a new course for the company. An action plan was set in motion by the top management and in October 2004, Kjeld was comfortable handing over the reins to a new CEO. In his own words:

> My job since January (2004) has been to change the course of the company and produce a blueprint for leading the LEGO Group back to profitability. We've charted our course – and we're well on our way. This is therefore the right moment to hand over control to the future managers of the company. As owner, I shall naturally continue to stay close to the company – as vice chairman of the board of LEGO Group and in my current capacity of chairman of the LEGO Foundation.[4]

New Chief Executive Officer – And New Challenges

Kjeld Kirk Kristiansen and the LEGO Group board chose an internal appointee as the right man to steer the company out of the crisis. Jørgen Vig Knudstorp was appointed the new chief executive officer. Jørgen Vig Knudstorp joined the LEGO Group in 2001 and, after being appointed CEO, immediately launched a new strategy for the company, building upon the action plan launched in early 2004. He had limited management experience when he took over as CEO, but in the view of company owner Kjeld Kirk Kristiansen, he had something more important than experience. He understood the LEGO philosophy and the thinking and attitudes behind it.

In an interview in the LEGO Group house magazine, the new CEO spoke of his new role:

> It's a natural continuation of my present role and the tasks I've tackled. I'm delighted to be working for the LEGO Group, and it's a great challenge helping to turn the ship around and getting the LEGO Group back into its natural position as market leader.[4]

Jørgen Vig Knudstorp was CEO of the LEGO Group from 2004 until 2017. During this period, the company regained focus on its core competencies and managed an impressive turnaround followed by more than a decade of continuous growth culminating with the LEGO Group becoming the world's largest toy company in 2015. This success included a vigorous expansion outside of the original Billund workshops to international plants worldwide with a focus on standardizing processes in order to control production. Efforts at reducing the complexity and the number of unique LEGO elements and focusing on supply chain planning were a strong start at managing this situation. One significant initiative was the planned and deployed Global Learning Center of Excellence utilizing the Training Within Industry (TWI) Job Instruction methodology to describe, document, and train core job knowledge and skills. I, the author of this book, was the leader of this effort and documented this journey in my book *Building a Global Learning Organization: Using TWI to Succeed with Strategic Workforce Expansion in the LEGO Group* (CRC Press, 2014).

The cycle came to a close in 2017 when the LEGO Group reported its first drop in sales and profits in more than a decade. This was the point in time when the company had to radically rethink its brand growth strategy to compete with challengers in, for example, digital offerings. The problem the company faced was weaker demand in established markets such as the US and parts of Europe where a saturation point had been reached.

Preparing for Future Growth with New Transformation Initiatives

The overarching ambition in preparing for future growth involved reaching more children in existing markets, adding new brand experiences to our offering, and entering new markets. Finding new markets meant going where children had never had a LEGO play experience, for example in Asia, Latin America, and Africa. Making this a reality would involve a big transformation of the company because, in 2018, 90 percent of sales were in markets that contained only 10 percent of the world's children.

So new initiatives were launched aiming at preparing the LEGO Group for future growth. As CEO Jørgen Vig Knudstorp put it:

> For a global organization like ours, the need for change is constant and one we have not focused on or sufficiently invested in until now. We need to transform the company to manage transformations more effectively and on a bigger scale than ever before. Going forward, we will take a big leap in the way we lead and operate our company. Over the last decade, we have seen tremendous growth and success. We can be proud of that. Unfortunately, we have also experienced growing pains. Our organization is stretched and we need to build leadership and organizational capabilities and capacity to handle future growth. It is about unleashing our potential – as an organization and as individuals.[4]

Establishing a New Corporate Management Area – The Need for Change

One of the initiatives was a leadership program that would equip the company and LEGO leaders to fulfill this potential through building capabilities and capacity throughout the organization. The crux of the program was to ensure that the LEGO Group's organization and leadership structure was strengthened to best enable the company's future growth and globalization. This also came with the objective of making the organization more "change ready" – to be mobilized to manage change as a constant element.

In order to ensure a successful implementation of the leadership program, a new Corporate Management area was established to support the transformation. This area was responsible for driving the program and a number of functions that were incorporated to support organizational and capability building in the company. Key focus aspects in this new area were building leadership capabilities to lead transformations and creating an approach for sustainable capability building to help execute the new Business Plan.

It was all about getting the right capabilities in place in order to facilitate getting LEGO bricks into the hands of more children. This involved closing current capability gaps, building capabilities for the future, and ensuring prioritization of projects in the portfolio – in other words, to focus on the right things first to deliver the Business Plan. Many things in the company had to be transformed as it was growing into a much bigger company with already existing growing pains. And this is where I, as the author, came into the picture. After finishing up my stint in creating and running the Global Learning Center, I was transferred to this new function to focus on leadership development and building an organization that is prepared and ready for change.

Building Sustainable Capabilities to Lead and Drive Transformations

The goal of the team was to define a structured approach for building capabilities in the LEGO Group in a way that combines leadership, people, function, and technology. The mission was not only to have all the right tools and processes in place when building capabilities but also to build the right skills and knowledge while having the right governance in place in order to develop the ability to handle transformations and meet the ambition of reaching many more children around the world with LEGO products.

In order to assess and drive change readiness across the organization, one of the key functions was transformation and the key priority here was building leadership capabilities. The direction was to make change "business as usual" and the norm at the LEGO Group ensuring that the company and its leaders are not only able to handle transformations but also to lead transformations in more effective and impactful ways. The framework for doing this involved leading through the LEGO essentials: The LEGO Brand Framework,[5] the Operating Model, and the Strategic Priorities.

The Leadership Program kicked off by targeting senior leaders and their direct reports and was a big multi-year program with the aim of equipping this community of leaders with skills to lead through transformations and growth in a global environment. The first two years of our efforts were fully dedicated to the Leadership Program that included development of coaching, feedback, and other relevant leadership skills. We were a team of six allocated specialists within the fields of learning, leadership development, change management, and communication, tasked with both designing and executing the different leadership modules. And we were leading and implementing the Leadership Program for the top 200 senior company leaders.

In 2018, after two years of intense roll-out of the program, the Executive Leadership Team changed and so did the focus on the program which shifted toward being fully dedicated to transformations and the development of the LEGO

Way of Change[6] as there was a clear acknowledgment that the need for change is constant and, therefore, a desire to invest more efforts in this. The objective was to have a common approach to leading transformations and guidance on how to navigate in uncertain and ambiguous times.

At the same time, changes took place in top management. In 2017, Niels Bjørn Christiansen was brought into the LEGO Group as CEO. With significant experience in digitalization, globalization, and the creation of agile and effective organizations, not to mention strong experience in transforming global companies, he understood the challenges that the LEGO Group was facing. Additionally, he brought with him a deep understanding of leadership in a family-owned, values-based, and purpose-driven company.

The Path Forward

This brief historical introduction and the outline of transformations, small and big, that occurred in the LEGO history is merely a humble but inspirational bite of the story of the amazing LEGO Group. With many years of consecutive growth and the ability to reach even more children around the globe, the LEGO Group continues to produce new and better results every year outpacing the toy industry and growing consumer sales, revenue, profit, and market share in all our major markets.

What is more, the COVID-19 pandemic created an even higher demand for LEGO products driven by children and families turning to play to help them through lockdowns and isolation. In this way the company has had great opportunities to inspire and develop even more builders of tomorrow which, as we have seen, were the same patterns and trends that the company faced during World War II.

The strong LEGO Values and LEGO Brand Framework are really brought to life as the LEGO Group plays an important part in building a sustainable future and creating a brighter world for our children to inherit. By joining forces with children and parents, employees, partners, NGOs, and experts, the company will have a lasting impact and inspire the children of today to become the builders of tomorrow.

LEGO Brand Framework

Through many years of growth, expansion, and transformation, it has been essential for the company to help all LEGO entities realize the company's vision. The LEGO Brand Framework created in 2008 set a clear path and a north star in the development and design of different elements of the LEGO Way of Change concept.

Briefly, the LEGO Brand Framework is the LEGO Group's mindset on the brand and the values attached to it. The LEGO Group formulated the LEGO Brand Framework and its four promises to its key stakeholders and the community at large: Play Promise, Partner Promise, Planet Promise, and People Promise. The LEGO Brand Framework shows clearly and unequivocally, in addition to the four promises, what the Group's vision, mission, spirit, and values are, thus gathering the whole ethos of the LEGO brand in one place.

The LEGO Brand Framework is to this day the essence of who the company is. The LEGO Group is a purpose-driven company, and the ultimate mission is to inspire and develop the builders of tomorrow by helping children to think creatively, reason systematically, and release their full potential in shaping their own futures. To deliver on the mission, the four promises have been defined through the LEGO Brand Framework which is the foundation for the strategy that identifies certain challenges and delivers intentional choices of where, how, and when to compete. According to Jørgen Vig Knudstorp in 2009:

> With the LEGO Brand Framework we are putting into words what the LEGO brand promises our stakeholders. We make very clear the values we promise everyone we interact with – whether they are colleagues, partners in retail, the wider community or – most important of all, of course – the children we deeply care for.[7]

Through tremendous growth, organizational changes, and a generally turbulent time, the framework has proven to be stable in a very dynamic world, and it is still functioning exactly as when it was launched. This is constantly being confirmed through feedback from leaders in various business areas, such as in a Change Leadership Training we had with new LEGO leaders coming from external companies where the focus was on how to handle teams being impacted by re-organizations. One of the new leaders expressed, "I really see the LEGO Values shine through in this approach." That was one of the best forms of feedback we can get when working with and rolling out the LEGO Way of Change as we succeed in translating the LEGO Values and the People Promise into tactical change initiatives and ways of leading the organization. The LEGO Brand Framework tells a lot about how we want to be as a company and it provides a lot of insight and guidance for employees into the company culture. Here is an overview of the LEGO Brand Framework – Figure 1.1.

Belief	Children are our role models			
Mission	Inspire and develop the builders of tomorrow			
Vision	A global force for Learning-through-Play			
Idea	System-in-Play			
Values	Imagination • Fun • Creativity • Caring • Learning • Quality			
Promises	Play Promise Joy of building, Pride of creation	People Promise Succeed together	Partner Promise Mutual value creation	Planet Promise Positive impact
Spirit	Only the best is good enough			

Figure 1.1 The LEGO Brand Framework

The LEGO Brand Framework is really about the spirit and the values which form the foundation of the culture, and there is a lot engrained here from the LEGO history. The Framework is active and alive in the organization being quoted and referred to in the daily dialogues of things like townhall meetings and reflections. A key element of the LEGO Brand Framework is the "4 Promises." A promise is seen as a handshake, which is more than just an intention. It is something you can live up to – or not live up to – and it is something you can exceed. The promises are made for all stakeholders who are important to us as a company and describe what they can expect from the LEGO Group as a company. Let me explain the People Promise as the most relevant for this context.

People Promise: Succeeding Together

The People Promise embodies the notion that the LEGO brand and company are no more than the people who represent it. It describes the give and the get of being an employee in the LEGO Group – what is expected of us and what are our opportunities. This is, in its essence, to seek to hire people with a strong fit to the LEGO culture, organizational principles, and LEGO values in order to develop an extraordinary and effective organization capable of delivering on its high ambitions and mission. It means a spirit of constantly seeking to do better, seeking the best where it matters the most, continuing to deepen capabilities within the LEGO system of play, and being as coherent as the LEGO building system in the way we work together.

How to Read This Book

Usually, a story is told in a linear way – you start at the beginning and keep going forward, systematically, until you come to the end. However, when telling the story of how the LEGO approach to manage and lead change was developed, there were many moving parts that, while occurring simultaneously, cannot be explained clearly or concisely at the same time. As an example, the approach and the framework of change were already well into the design and development process when the need for testing out the Simplify to Grow pilot initiative came up. And even as we ran a pilot and created a context within which to test and learn, as well as demonstrate the effectiveness of the new methodology, the change team was still creating and adjusting the approach to find the right balance and fit to the organization.

So the book is divided into sections to explain the different aspects of the entire project: laying the groundwork, the pilot project, creating the change approach along with experiences and learnings in the practice.

Part I: Laying the Groundwork

Part I, which we have just covered here, reviews the historical view of the LEGO transformations over the company's long history to provide an understanding of the context and the situation the company found itself in when realizing the need for change – and the "burning platform" that created the need for an approach to leading change. It covers how the approach to managing and leading changes in the LEGO Way is connected to the LEGO Promises and thereby the LEGO Values as key objectives. Additionally, it looks at how the change approach was developed, the initial steps that were taken in relation to the big leap of the company, and how a new corporate area was established to prepare for future growth.

Part II: The Pilot Case – Simplify to Grow

In Part II of the book, we move toward the more specific context of the pilot project and the practical approaches that were taken in relation to the LEGO transformation: "Simplify to Grow." We describe how this transformation was designed and executed and, while not getting into all the specific details of what changed in the company due to the transformation, what key learning points were obtained in relation to how we were managing and leading the change. We discuss the major change activities that were brought into play and why these were selected to be the foundation for the "Simplify to Grow" initiative that was considered as a pilot initiative, providing a good context for testing the different approaches to the LEGO Way of Change.

Part III: Launching the LEGO Way of Change in the Organization

Part III makes up the bulk of the book and provides more details on the LEGO Way of Change, and how to deploy this approach in an organizational context. The LEGO Way of Change is based and founded on five "Moments that Matter": Getting Ready,

Understanding the Change, Personalizing the Change, Navigating the Change, and Living the Change. Here you will find guides on how to use the different tools and interventions, and specific cases and stories telling how LEGO leaders have worked with the different approaches and their learnings along the way. Here you find insightful guides drawing on behavioral science.

Part IV: Conclusion and Visionary View of the Future

This last part will include a conclusion and a visionary view of the way forward.

Who Is This Book For?

This book is ideal for audiences leading and driving change and transformations. It could simply be individuals being passionate and interested in the topic, or being predominantly in the following roles:

- Change and transformation leaders (business/people leaders)
- Project managers
- Change practitioners
- Continuous improvement specialists
- Human resource business partners
- Organization development professionals

Throughout the book, you will be inspired and disrupted in your thinking through tools, know-how, and leader experiences that you will need to drive successful transformations going forward. I hope you will be encouraged and ready to test and learn some of the tools and approaches, thereby developing your leadership capabilities and accelerating your impact in leading and managing the people side of change.

Transformation vs. Change – What Is the Difference?

Before reading the book, it is relevant to understand my view on Transformation vs. Change, and what the difference is.

Being aware of and understanding the differences between transformation and change will support and guide you on your way to moving forward in the best way. This understanding will also show you how to dose your efforts accordingly. The two concepts tend to get lumped together, and they may seem like the same thing. No doubt the concepts are closely connected, but there are differences.

Change (also known as Change Management) refers to implementing a finite initiative or set of connected initiatives – to make a clear, measurable shift in specific aspects that are clear and well-defined. Here, the focus could be on processes, ways of working, and procedures to achieve a particular goal – for example, if you want to improve a specific process around commercial planning and introduce a new software to support this. So here, change is concrete and defined.

Transformation, on the other hand, is a larger concept. If change is about shifting something within the business, transformation is more about shifting the company and the culture of the company, often based on bigger strategic initiatives and directions. It is about reinventing the way the organization does business and often includes overall behavioral changes. Transformation is often a larger and more complex initiative, more overarching and with a longer duration.

Both change and transformation will impact the organization, and change initiatives will be more straightforward to identify as they happen. In transformation, you are looking to transform the organization and there will be many moving parts to enable the shift, some strategic and some tactical.

Whether the initiatives you are working on are characterized by a set of well-defined changes – or are more a full-blown organizational transformation, the steps you can take to successfully lead and drive the shifts in leadership practices have commonalities. As an example, no matter if it is a well-defined change or a more complex transformation, it is essential to create a vision to set the direction and to provide purpose and the "why" that is ambitious and compelling and serves as the foundation and north star for all the activities that follow. Without a direction and a vision, there is no clear aim and change is likely to fail.

The same goes for the other tools and approaches included in this book. They are targeted toward both change and transformation based on the focus on people that is similar, whether it is smaller simple change or bigger complex transformation.

Notes

1. The most powerful Brands – The Most Powerful Brands in 2017 (forbes.com).
2. About the LEGO Group – A new reality – LEGO® History – LEGO.com US.
3. About the LEGO Group – Godtfred Kirk Christiansen – LEGO® History – LEGO.com US.
4. About the LEGO Group: Management – The LEGO Group – About us – LEGO.com US.
5. On page 9 – the LEGO Brand Framework is further explained.
6. The LEGO Way of Change is a change framework providing a common approach to how to design, lead, and anchor change in a thoughtful, effective, and impactful way. You will find a detailed intro to the LEGO Way of Change in Chapter 3.
7. About the LEGO Brand: The LEGO Brand – The LEGO Group – About us – LEGO.com US.

CHAPTER 2

SIMPLIFY TO GROW
Initial Pilot to Test and Learn

In 2017, the LEGO Group® reported its first drop in sales and profits in more than a decade. This was the point of time when the company had to radically rethink its brand growth strategy to compete with challengers in, for example, digital product offerings that were redefining the toy marketplace. The problem for the LEGO Group was weaker demand in established markets, such as the US and parts of Europe, where the saturation point for its products had been reached.

In the five years leading up to this point, the LEGO Group had invested in massive growth. Both the workforce and the number of product lines offered had grown tremendously, and this had left the company over-extended. Stock was piling up in warehouses and there just was not enough room on the store shelves. The toy market is all about what is new, so the only way to move the stock was by reducing the price – devaluing the brand in the process.

Jørgen Vig Knudstorp stated in a press release,

> We have added complexity into the organization, which now makes it harder for us to grow further. As a result, we have pressed the reset-button for the entire group.[1]

The key focus in 2017 was to stabilize the top line by regaining market momentum through root-cause analyses of problems and addressing stall-outs that were stifling growth and, at the same time, removing organizational complexity. The direction for 2018/2019+ was to build growth drivers in the markets and achieve organizational effectiveness that would continuously drive for speed, simplicity, productivity, and ownership.

This resulted in cutting 1,400 jobs – about 12–13% of the monthly paid employees in the global workforce. In addition, 50% of employees would have a new manager after the transformation – though this restructuring would prepare the company to grow back stronger. The top management was also restructured, and the next leadership layer below was changed and went through the same process

DOI: 10.4324/9781003243113-2

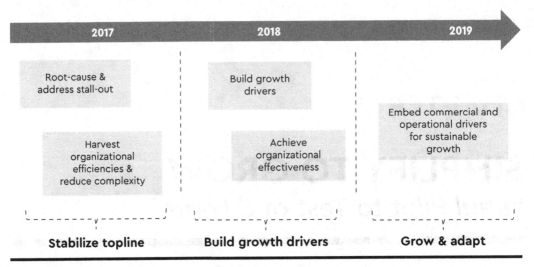

Figure 2.1   The "Simplify to Grow" initiative.

as the rest of the organization. The idea was to build a smaller and less complex organization to simplify the LEGO business model in order to reach more children. This would also impact costs as the reset in the markets meant a clean-up of inventories across the entire value chain.

At this point in time, the LEGO Group faced two critical challenges: firstly, commercial stall-out caused by top-line stagnation, competitors catching up, and lack of root-cause clarity, and secondly, organizational indigestion due to complexity and oversized organization, as referred to in Figure 2.1.

Based on this situation, the "Simplify to Grow" initiative was launched with the purpose of taking action to reestablish the trajectory of achieving the mission to "Inspire and develop builders of tomorrow… and reach 300 million children by 2032."

The leadership team clearly pointed out that Simplify to Grow was about getting the organization in shape and investing in the right areas and capabilities for future growth, for example, digital vs. more traditional IT or planning capabilities to drive long-term growth, allowing the company to achieve its mission.

Objectives and Design Principles of the Simplify to Grow Initiative

Rightsizing was a critical step on the journey to simplifying the organization with the objectives of improving overall organizational effectiveness through increased speed, simplicity, innovation, ownership, and improving productivity to ultimately address the commercial challenges being faced.

To ensure consistency across the different business units, design principles were laid out:

■ Further build distinct competitive advantage – no cookie-cutter approach
■ Ensure delivery of defined priorities
■ Protect long-term core capabilities and non-negotiables.

The Approach and How to Deliver

The Executive Leadership Team had the ownership, accountability, and direction-setting throughout the program. Additionally, their respective leadership teams were deeply involved and co-created solutions.

A project team was staffed with fully dedicated LEGO people. Here sub-teams were established for each leadership area. One team consisted of a Business Representative, Human Resource Partner, Executive Strategy & Agenda Representative, as well as external consultants. Additionally, the teams were supported by representatives of Human Resource Analytics, Change Management, Communications, and Finance who acted as counterparts to external consultancy support to ensure organizational anchoring and speed. These teams were responsible for analyzing and designing the organization within each area. Recommendations would be shared with the Executive Leadership Team for final decision.

Different Phases of Implementation Delivery

The timeline of the program was divided into three distinct phases in a focused 3-month process to manage organizational motivation.

The first phase was to build a fact-based analysis and direction setting with a key deliverable to be baseline diagnostic of opportunities and challenges to de-layering the organization. This baseline was carried out through interviews and data insights throughout the first month of activity.

The second phase was to decide on the new organization design. Here the key deliverable was the new organizational design down to position level, and additionally, to identify productivity improvement opportunities both within and across each leadership area.

The third and last phase was planning and mobilization of the organization with the outcome of having transformation, communication, and HR transition plans in place. This was to be followed by the implementation.

All phases and the implementation were to be supported by ongoing transformation management and communication activities. This initiative offered a huge opportunity to test and pilot the LEGO Way of Change concept for the first time. At the same time, it was a large-scale transformation as it impacted the entire LEGO organization.

CASE STUDY: SIMPLIFY TO GROW

By Kasper Thams, Transformation Director

One of the key drivers of this transformation was Kasper Thams, Transformation Director in Strategy & Transformation. Here are his views and learnings from this transformation where the LEGO Way of Change was piloted and tested:

> We had a clear focus on not cutting costs and people, but looking into simplifying the organization. The focus was on three key areas: first, to remove unnecessary activities and reduce complexity. The company had only grown organically, so there was a big focus on teams that had been built up, doing the same or similar activities, but being anchored in different parts of the organization. Secondly, to remove middle management offices that did not add value. The third part was the number of leaders, as the ratio between leaders and employees was too high in several areas. Workstreams were set up to look into those three areas and to come up with recommendations and future options. This approach was significantly different from other, more traditional approaches to rightsizing in organizations, where you focus on removing costs and setting targets for each business area, for example, how can we cut away 100 jobs in a specific area.
>
> Based on this direction, interviews were conducted to come up with suggestions on how to qualify and drive the transformation and which positions to take out from the organization. This was more difficult to do in theory than in practice, so at some point in time, we had to adjust our approach and manage the number of positions to reduce by area while keeping the objectives in mind. By then, the working team had outlined various options and needed direction on how much and where to make changes. As such, it ended up being a blend of rightsizing and reorganization where teams were merged and positions were removed in order to streamline the areas that needed it. This was still all done based on data and findings from interviews where complexities and overlapping functions were discovered.

Strong Orchestration

The transformation required strong orchestration as the whole company was impacted. Thams explains how the process was managed:

> In parallel with the interviews and deep dives into the different functional areas, we had a weekly cadence, where business leads together with HR reported back on status, their findings, and progress. Each organizational area was led by senior business leaders who allocated 100% of their time to this initiative. The weekly status, new findings, and challenges were consolidated across teams

and shared first with the head of Transformation and the head of HR – and then with the full Executive Leadership Team including the CEO. Often the Chairman of the Board would also join the discussions. All happened on a weekly cadence with plenty of touchpoints so it required a lot of orchestration – particularly when we came closer to the announcement. This was a big puzzle, as all employees would have individual 1:1 dialogues with their leaders, and we needed to plan the sequence of these meetings so similar teams and individuals would be told at the same time to avoid misaligned communication and misunderstandings.

To be consistent across the business areas, we had defined three different levels of impact. In the dialogue with your leader, you could get the message that (1) there are no changes in relation to your role, (2) you still have a role but there are changes, e.g., a new leader or changes to the setup of your team or areas of responsibility, or (3) there is no role for you in the new setup. In the latter case, the process of layoffs and support packages was initiated. All individuals across the group had this type of dialogue with their leaders.

It was a big coordination task to ensure that you did not hear about the outcome from another team before you were told about the impact on your own team. From May 'till October, we were working on opportunities for each area, people being impacted, process changes, etc.' It may seem like a long period of time from the outside, but for the task force it was very compressed. There is a lot of complexity, evaluation of options, etc. that you do not see when you are not part of it, and with people being impacted, there was extreme focus on making the best possible decisions.

A clear decision was taken on communicating early to be in line with the LEGO Group expectations and culture of being open and transparent. However, it created a lot of uncertainty in the entire organization and drove the perception that the initiative took a very long time. In addition, many townhalls with limited news or no news at all created an impatience in the organization. On the contrary, people recognized the openness and intent. The intention of communicating openly and early was good; however, it built up pressure on the entire process. If this had not been communicated up-front, the alternative would have been rumors and corridor-talk about what was going on. There is no perfect approach – it is important to be clear on trade-offs and decisions.

Transformation Activities Being Critical

Many people were involved in the transformation task force from various business areas, the HR organization, and the Strategy & Transformation Team. Everybody worked hard over the summer. "It was a tough environment," Thams mentions.

For many, their position was at stake and they knew it. Many tough discussions were happening daily, having both rational and emotional dimensions, and working with such tight deadlines in a tough program, friction was unavoidable. We could have considered more proactively how to handle these frictions, but the time pressure made it difficult. That said, the change activities were very important as so many people were involved. In addition, it was a significant task to make sure that all leaders involved were prepared to take the dialogues with people being impacted and make sure that these people were understanding the rationale behind the decisions.

Another challenge was to manage how people would maintain the same level of knowledge. There were differences in how much leaders could share with individuals and it was difficult for us to control what people in the organization were aware of what. Occasionally we had to involve more people in selected areas to make sure that the right solutions were designed, and so we needed to bring people with deeper knowledge closer to the solution design.

Leader Mobilization

The scaling of this was critical. We needed to get as many leaders as possible ready for the implementation, and they needed to be trained in the LEGO Way of Change, which is described in detail in the next part of this book. In other words, they should be prepared for employee dialogues and be prepared to handle those dialogues with the people being impacted in different ways. Often they would only find out about the future of their own position shortly before having to tell their teams.

There were strategic discussions about what levels of leaders should have leadership training. The time allotted would only allow for top Level 1–3 leaders to go through the training, even though many leaders below that level would be conducting the dialogues with their employees. So that was a critical trade-off the team had to make.

However, it worked well that there were both open training sessions with leaders across different teams and also specific Leadership Team sessions for each area. It quickly became clear, as well, that there were different maturity levels among the teams, so we had to adjust the process to focus more effort on the areas that needed preparation the most.

Another thing we learned was that after the announcements, many employees were left with a feeling of emptiness and uncertainty about the next steps. The leaders were given the task to follow up with individuals and teams but the degree of the follow-up varied. In addition, a challenge was for leaders to bring back focus and a feeling of psychological safety to the employees untouched by the rightsizing, which was not always easy.

Here is an overview of the different leadership levels (Figure 2.2).

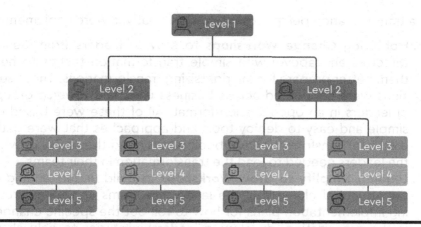

Figure 2.2 Organizational leadership levels.

The Pilot Case – The LEGO Way of Change

This was the point in time when the LEGO Way of Change was introduced for the first time – and, in the context of Simplify to Grow, it was a very relevant, strong, and intense environment to test it in and to demonstrate impact. There was a big appetite, need, and demand to get the LEGO leaders prepared for the transformation. As a starting point of the full LEGO Way of Change approach, with all the tools that we had developed, we designed a tailored package of the relevant elements for the Simplify to Grow initiative. Different interventions and leader sessions were conducted for leaders who needed it most, and when they needed it most.

In the "Getting-Ready" mobilization workshops for leaders, the initial part of the LEGO Way of Change, there was focus on the leaders' role during the transformation, the importance of authentic engagement, role modeling, managing resistance, and how to have courageous conversations with individuals being impacted. The aim was to mobilize the leaders through a series of experiences and tools that would help them to lead, manage, and engage with teams as they navigated through the changes ahead of them.

In these sessions, we had our hands tied, to some extent, because we could not talk in specifics about the changes taking place in the different areas, as there was no awareness of the full impact of what was coming. At the same time, we needed to handle the communication flow and confidentiality. Based on the different levels of knowledge among the leaders, we used the metaphor of a flight simulator. In order to set expectations and to be clear that no specifics would be shared, but on the contrary, to prepare and give as much support as possible to deal with all possible eventualities, we likened the process to flying through a storm where we would prepare the leaders for the worst, even though many would never encounter this in reality, only in the "simulator." Additionally, it was called out clearly that the sessions were not meant to turn leaders into transformation experts but to focus on providing leaders with practical, tactical skills and tools to help them in leading the transformation process.

From a transformation perspective, two key initiatives were implemented:

1. **Mobilizing Change Workshops** to provide leaders (from Senior Directors and above) with simple transformation tactics to help them better prepare for the rightsizing transformations. Those sessions were conducted across business units with diverse groups of leaders in an open session format. All of these were based on simple and easy-to-deploy tools and approaches that were gathered in a Transformation Playbook that formed the basics of what the leaders needed to lead the transformation in their teams.

2. **Leading Simplify to Grow Workshops** to build understanding of the structural changes in the leadership teams as well as creating implementation plans for how to roll out the specific changes in the organization, developing leadership stories to help share the direction the specific area was going, and finally creating an engagement plan for the area. Those sessions were conducted for each leadership team in the specific business units.

In addition to the mobilizing workshops, online follow-up sessions with optional attendance were offered. Below in Figure 2.3, is an overview of the different elements of the two approaches.

	Mobilizing Change Workshops	**Leading Simplify to Grow Workshops**
Objectives	To provide leaders with simple change tools to help them being prepared for the rightsizing changes	To come together as a new team – and to create understanding of the structural cascaded changes – and create implementation and engagement plans
Format	Across business units – open format	In leadership teams in their respective areas
Key Themes	• What is Change leadership? • Understanding the change – change starts with self • Communication and engagement • Prepare your change story • Emotional reactions to change • Prepare courageous conversation	• Where are you on your personal change journey? • Implementation planning – defining key activities and responsibilities • Create area specific story lines

Figure 2.3 Change Workshops formats and themes.

Key Learnings from the Pilot

The LEGO Way of Change was really tested thoroughly with 300+ leaders in very diverse groups of leaders from development, operations, sales, and administrative areas. And what worked well was that the key elements were tailored to the unique situations of the leaders involved on each team, so it was really contextualized in the rightsizing initiative.

Timing

The workshops were carried out at the "point-of-time" which was 2–3 weeks before the announcements of the specific changes. There was a need for the leaders to get specific guidance on how and what to prepare for these announcements and the sessions also allowed and encouraged the leaders to internalize and understand the transformation. The individual levels of knowledge of the change were quite different from leader to leader. Some were 100% aware of what was going to happen while others had not heard anything about the coming changes. But with good timing of the leader mobilization sessions, the leaders had 2–3 weeks to get up to the needed knowledge level, to internalize and prepare their change story, and to prepare for individual one-on-one meetings with their employees in the short time allotted.

As a leader, you always hope to be involved as early as possible in situations like these, but with the cascading changes going on in all areas of the organization and the need for informing top levels of management of the changes first, there was limited time for most of the leaders to get up to speed. So there were big differences in the levels of uncertainty of leaders in the different sessions depending on their level of involvement and the impact. In fact, many of the leaders were impacted by the change personally.

Involvement of People Leaders

In general, it was a challenge to design and ensure that the "right" people were participating in the training sessions organizationally without involving the next level of leaders, in this case Level 4 and 5 leaders. This created dissatisfaction and gave those leaders a still shorter time to internalize the changes that were then communicated to them very late in the process. Additionally, not including Level 4 and 5 in the workshops was a challenge as many of the dialogues with employees were going to be initiated by leaders at these levels. To compensate for the lack of leader workshop participation, online sessions were offered for all leaders. However, not many leaders took the time and the opportunity to join the online sessions to upscale their leadership skills as they were too busy understanding the change, the impact it had on themselves as leaders, and the impact it had on their teams. Therefore, there was also an opportunity to include the Level 3 leaders in the dialogues with employees, together with their direct leaders, which many chose to do.

Primarily Looking at Organizational Structure

Another learning from the pilot initiative was that, due to the size and scale of the transformation, it ended up with primary focus on organizational structure and not on ways of working and changing behaviors. There was ample support to the leaders in relation to the announcement of the change and to make sure that this was done in a good LEGO Way in line with our People Promise. However, much more effort, support, and facilitation on how to implement, mobilize, and make the new organization sustainable could have been done. Activities like designing new ways of working and defining desired behaviors in the new setups were really underestimated and not supported to the extent needed to make the change stick. This learning was brought into the way we do transformations today where we, as transformation leaders, are supporting the business areas in leading and managing the transformation over a longer and more focused period of time. This is to ensure that we are getting into the deeper layers of the transformation and investing in understanding the case for change, current behaviors, and what new desired behaviors are needed to succeed and to make the transformation stick. You will find much more inspiration on those essential elements in Part III of this book.

Many of the learnings and experiences from the Simplify to Grow pilot project were included and integrated into the Strategy and Transformation practice, where we today are bringing LEGO Strategies to life through the LEGO Way of Change approach. These are going hand-in-hand with other approaches like project management and agile ways of working. By tailoring the best suited transformational approach to the specific strategy implementation and its related business context, we optimize the conditions for creating value through our transformation practices and making new behaviors stick in the organization.

Note

1. Lego to cut 1,400 jobs as sales slide – BBC News. https://www.nbcnews.com/business/business-news/lego-cut-1–400-jobs-after-decades-long-sales-boom-n798716

CHAPTER 3

CREATING THE LEGO®
WAY OF CHANGE

In this part of the book, you will be introduced to the LEGO Way of Change (LWOC), which is an approach and a framework consisting of experiences, guides, and tools that we bring into play when working with transformations in the LEGO Group. The LWOC was developed with the objective of creating one unified approach through a common understanding and a common language to transformation and change, and to provide leaders leading transformations and practitioners with experiences and tools that they can bring into play with a strong focus on the people side of the transformation. Additionally, it was developed with the intent of creating a thinking, focus, and curiosity that change is not something we have to endure, but rather something we should naturally embrace and use to grow.

As described in the last chapter, with the Simplify to Grow initiative, we were in a situation with many different views and approaches to change. We had smaller communities in the company being trained in different approaches and others were applying their approaches and framework activities based on their individual experiences. So by having this common approach we sought to be more efficient and synergized in our change approach. That being said, it's a journey that we are still on. We are deploying the LWOC in larger, prioritized strategic transformations with the intent of scaling to a wider segment and more broadly in the LEGO community.

The LWOC was created in close collaboration with MindGym[1] which specializes in behavior change. Together and in close collaboration, we have translated behavioral science principles into a unique set of experiences, practical guides, and tools that align with the LEGO business. MindGym's behavioral research-based approach combined with our understanding of the LEGO business and the LEGO culture has resulted in this approach being very well in line with the LEGO People Promise, which was an important design criterion. We focused on experiences with a very human-centered way of always doing our best to do transformation

DOI: 10.4324/9781003243113-3

and change WITH people and not TO people. Additionally, the LWOC is a leader-led approach. Leaders play a vital and important role as they are the closest link between the organization and its employees – they are *leading* the organization. So in the role of change practitioners, for the vast majority of the time we are coaching, mentoring, sparring, and mobilizing leaders to lead the change, making sure that the experiences, products, and tools of the LWOC are landing well in the LEGO organization when creating company-wide behavior change.

Change Leadership AND Change Management Matter

There is no doubt that Change Management has been out of fashion for a long time. However, change must be well managed and it also requires effective leadership to be successful. In the LWOC, you will see an integrated approach reflecting cognitive, emotional, and behavioral dimensions. Changes and trans-formations must be well organized, planned, and directed, and, at the same time, it also requires effective leadership to introduce, lead, and sustain change suc-cessfully. Change Management typically refers to a set of basic tools, processes, or structures intended to keep any change effort under control and minimize problems. So with Change Management, the goal is often to minimize the disrup-tions and to ensure that the change is done efficiently by keeping things under control and assuring that the planned change stays within, for example, budget and schedule.

Change Leadership is fundamentally different. It harnesses the energy and the power of people, other driving forces, visions, and interventions that fuel large-scale and sustainable transformation.

In the LWOC, you will see that there are aspects of both management and leadership. For example, management in the LWOC includes analyzing who will be impacted by the change, how they will be impacted, and how big the impact is. By creating communication and engagement plans and following up on change progression indicators, it ensures that the change is progressing.

The leadership aspects include how to inspire belief in the change and empower the organization to move toward a better future. Also, it shows how to bring the future state to life through a strong and clear vision with compelling storytelling and how you can find and empower the change catalysts in the organization. Depending on the specific business context, you can dose out and tailor the right mix of Change Management and Change Leadership.

There is a need to make the whole change journey go faster, smarter, and more efficiently to keep up with the pace of the world changing around us. This is aptly captured in the trendy managerial acronym, the *"VUCA World"* – a world characterized by "Volatility, Uncertainty, Complexity and Ambiguity." So Change Leadership is a challenge for the future as this is associated with the bigger leaps we have to make, those windows of opportunity that come at us faster, stay open for less time, and provide bigger hazards.

To become the organization we're aiming to be, we need to be ever ready, ever changing.

What Does "Change" Mean for Us?

Change Is Business as Usual

Change should be seen as a part of our everyday experience rather than a process with a clear start and finish. Although there are discrete change journeys within this progression to the future, it's not a linear process. Rather, it is an ever-evolving narrative.

Change Is Personal

Change is a distinctly individual experience, and it's important to recognize the human side of any transformation. Acknowledging the psychological and emotional impact will help us better understand how to support others through it. We need to put the personal back into the experience and allow people to take control and make it their own in order to alleviate feelings of anxiety and uncertainty.

Change Is an Opportunity

Change is an opportunity to embrace the inherent innovation and creativity of the LEGO Group – not just in terms of processes and practices but also to reach even more children around the world. By celebrating constant learning through curiosity, we can build an environment of confident uncertainty – one in which we thrive through change.

The LEGO Way of Change – Unfolding It Even More

We do not see change as a linear, sequential process taking us from points A to B. The reality is much messier; it's a journey, and an adventurous, unexpected one at that. We loop back, we stall, and we pivot, with everyone's experience being different. It is varied and unpredictable – it's all about adaptation. It's a different skill than managing and delivering a program or initiative that has a beginning and an end. What's more challenging and more common today is to be constantly agile in the face of emergent and complex, nonlinear and unpredictable change – both in the work and in the world at large.

In reality, it looks more like this:

Figure 3.1   The change journey.

It might look messy and unpredictable, but what is certain is that there are critical moments in this journey, times when circumstances and people's beliefs, knowledge, and feelings combine to create a potential turning point. We can turn these in favor of change.

Moments That Matter

What is a "moment that matters"? A moment that matters is a critical point in the journey where people's circumstances, beliefs, knowledge, and feelings create the potential for great success or possible failure. They are the points where leaders are most likely to intervene to boost success and safeguard the change journey. For each moment, we're ultimately concerned with directing people's emotions, moving them into the most positive, constructive place possible. The experiences and tools of the LWOC are focused on this, but there's also a continuous thread of building belief throughout.

A Hard and Fast Breakdown of a "Moment That Matters"

A "moment" may be elastic – it's not a single incident but a period during which critical factors come into play and occasionally return. They are not necessarily sequential as presented, but they will usually follow one from another. And different individuals may experience different moments simultaneously. Finally, the outcomes of each moment will create an impact on the moments of others. Here a visual overview of the Moments That Matter – Figure 3.2.

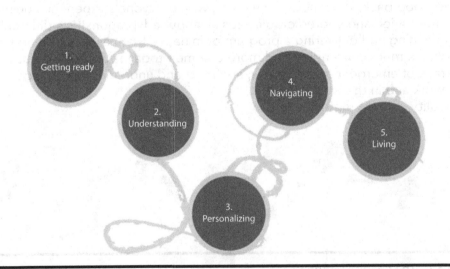

Figure 3.2 Moments that matter.

So What Are the Moments?

Throughout the journey, we want to be able to recognize these moments that matter and intervene with experiences, practical tools, advice, and coaching. In the next part of the book, you will find tactics, experiences, and interventions for each moment to help you navigate the change journey and you will also find case studies and stories from leaders having experienced and deployed those interventions. These are all designed to complement what already exists and what you already do to deliver successful changes and transformations.

Going into the Moments That Matter

1. **Getting Ready**
   The point where there is a clear need to change, but the details and exact purpose are not yet clear. Leaders are still considering options and looking for consensus, so the wider population is not yet involved.
2. **Understanding**
   When leaders agree on the high-level purpose of change or transformation, it's now time to dive into the specifics and build a plan for the right option to deliver that purpose.
3. **Personalizing**
   The point where all affected people make sense of the change and how it relates to their own motivations and aspirations. And this would also be where they know how they will be impacted by the change as an individual.
4. **Navigating**
   This is where planning meets reality, as change is being brought into daily life. The organization is rolling out a new way of working, with inevitable challenges and adaptations.
5. **Living**
   The new ways of working may have taken hold and people are committing to them – it's now becoming part of normal operations. People can reconnect with the purpose of the change and review what they've achieved.

What Happens in between Moments?

Although the moments that matter highlight the most critical points in a journey, it's important to stay connected to the process and maintain some level of involvement. Here are some inspirational ways to stay connected.

Staying Engaged

Between moments, maintain feedback loops and informal contacts at all levels of the organization. These will keep these connections live and provide a means to monitor progress without undue workload. The change catalysts are invaluable here, so we suggest arranging update meetings with them (as well as the relevant leaders) to keep up to date. There's no substitute for "going native," spending time among colleagues going through the change.

Looking for Signs

Use your connections to look for signals that the change is approaching a "moment that matters." That way you can anticipate and improve your chances of emerging with positive, powerful outcomes.

Leader Coaching

During the change process, leaders will look to you for advice on challenges and opportunities beyond those which arise during the "moments." Providing ongoing advice to support their change capability and role is essential to allow them to take the lead rather than just deferring to senior leaders when clarity or direction is required.

Be Authentic

Regardless of where you are in the journey, it's vitally important people believe in your conviction. Try to avoid showing people false optimism or cynical skepticism.

Note

1. Psychology Based Organisational Transformation | MindGym (themindgym.com).

CHAPTER 4

MOMENT 1 – GETTING READY

What Is It?

Getting ready to change is the point where there's a clear need to change, but the details and exact purpose are not yet clear. Leaders are still considering options and looking for consensus, so the wider population is not yet involved.

Possible Signs That Indicate We Need to Get Ready to Change

- Our business/function is not performing at the right level to deliver the results we need. This can be caused when the world around us is changing, e.g., new consumer patterns, the sustainable and digital agenda.
- We are recognizing opportunities to be even better at what we do. But don't know what this looks like.
- People are saying that it's time to change, but are vague or uncertain about what that change or transformation should be.
- We've noticed that we may be overcompensating for a process or aspect of the business that's not working properly and can be improved.

How People Are Feeling

- "I'm excited – I think we could be so much better!"
- "I'm certain – I know exactly what we need to change, let me tell you..."
- "I'm fine – no need to change anything here"
- "I'm frustrated – things need to change and soon"
- "I'm anxious – something's not quite right"

DOI: 10.4324/9781003243113-4

Why It Matters?

If we get this moment right, we'll get:

- A shared sense of direction and a vision of success
- A base of trust among business leaders
- A sense of being actively involved from senior stakeholders
- Involvement and collaboration at all levels

If we don't get it right:

- We won't have some people's permission to change
- There will be questionable alignment on the need and purpose
- Passionate people may charge off in the wrong direction
- We could get stuck talking about change, not making decisions, and not getting out of the starting blocks

WHERE AND HOW CAN YOU HAVE THE BIGGEST IMPACT?

- Educate key stakeholders in the LEGO Way of Change philosophy
- Involve people early and foster a collaborative approach to change
- Leverage self-awareness and understanding of the change to be ready to engage and communicate in an authentic way

Where	How
Help leaders understand the change through better self-awareness	**Change Starts with Self** page 32
Help leaders align around a clear vision and purpose	**Change Vision workshop** page 35

Change Starts with Self – *"We Need Not Wait to See What Others Do"*[1]

What Is It?

In the process of getting leaders aligned with and positive about the change and the ambition of this, and in preparation to getting started with, for example, crafting the vision, it can be useful to have a dialogue about the role of the leader with the objective of enhancing the self-awareness of the leaders. The situation would typically play out in a leadership team session where we introduce the change approach – what change leadership in action could look like and there could be a dialogue on what change experiences and interventions would be relevant in the specific context.

Why It Matters?

Here, it's relevant to emphasize that in order to lead the transformation it's important that leaders start with themselves and become aware of where they are in their own journeys. The success of the actions they take as leaders does *not* depend solely on what they do or how they do it, but on the self or the inner state from which they operate. The key to increasing their impact through the transformation is to "upgrade" and increase their self-awareness through exploring their inner world. This is the way to effectively lead yourself in order to effectively lead others.

Like it or not, people look to their leader, whether it is for answers, support, or to see what they are doing in response to a change. There will definitely be a need for leaders to engage with and enable change, but there's no avoiding the fact that, as a leader, you bear a heavier load along the journey. If one of the questions you sometimes ask is, "How do I get my people to change or support this change?" then you must first check whether you have changed yourself and if you're role modeling the change and showing support for the change. This can feel uncomfortable, challenging, and stretching, but remember this is how it's supposed to be. Change will always be a stretch – even leaders with extensive experience leading changes will feel stretched doing something new.

An element of self-awareness is to look into the role of the leader. Here you can create awareness around the multiple roles that you as a leader play in change and this can be hard. See Figure 4.1.

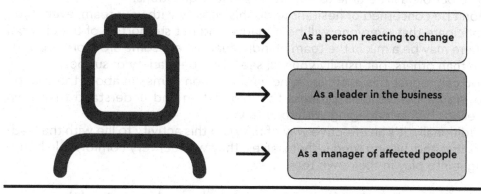

As a person reacting to change

As a leader in the business

As a manager of affected people

Figure 4.1   What is my leader role?

1. *You are, as a person or individual, reacting to change.* If you are impacted yourself, you have a different or a new role; letting go of team members or taking over new responsibilities could be examples of how you could be impacted yourself.
2. *You are in the role of leader managing affected people.* This requires that you inspire belief, empower, engage, and support your team.
3. *You are a leader in the business.* You ensure that the daily operations are running as usual and that products are delivered; in other words, you keep the business running even though changes are being made.

As a leader, you can easily feel torn between these different roles as the roles might contradict each other and there will be some trade-offs to make. It's important to take time out to understand how you feel about the change and your own perspective on it. How we act and interact with everyone will shape their perspective of the change.

In this way, we will be able to speak to our people without bringing in our own biases, but we must start by being aware of what they are. To help us become aware of our own biases as leaders, the following short activity is very useful to work through either individually or together in your leadership team. It is also a very good dialogue exercise that you can do with your team and it helps you work through your feelings about the change.

How to Bring It into Action

This exercise (Figure 4.2) can be done in multiple formats, face-to-face, in one-on-one coaching sessions, in teams, online, as a dialogue, or as a written exercise, but I have not experienced any limitations of this yet.

■ People like to be asked how they feel – it shows that you care about them. As a leader, you will get a lot of great insights into how your team is seeing, thinking, and feeling about the change. Treat this information as a treasure and bring it into play in your one-on-one follow-up dialogues. Get back with answers to the questions that you might not be able to answer in the session.
■ Give people a little time to reflect on the four questions.
■ Don't be concerned or hesitant to do this activity with your team, even if you anticipate that everyone will be negative and not supportive of the change. There may be a mix in the team of individuals where some are more supportive than others, but usually you will see a broader variety of support.
■ You can repeat this exercise as new information comes in about the change to ensure that leaders process the information and understand their own feelings before engaging with their teams.
■ Additionally, it's an effective way of bringing this activity to life with the leaders first and, having tried it themselves, they will feel very comfortable bringing it into play in their own teams.

It is important to allow time for leaders to internalize and understand the change – another important part of "Getting Ready" is to create a strong north star for the transformation.

What do you understand about the change? - exercise

Work through each of the 5 key questions then follow up with actions to help you move forward

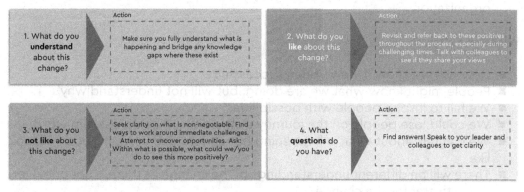

Figure 4.2 What do you understand about the change?

Crafting a Vision for Change – Vision Workshop

What Is It?

While we may know what people need to believe in about a change in order to accept it, there is no fixed formula for how to help a group of people change their minds. Sometimes, it can be as simple as a compelling communications campaign, strong townhall engagement sessions, or even a new app. But more likely, it will involve developing a unified point of view among leaders and then participating with people in dialogue around that point of view through different types of engagements, empowerments, and approaches.

A *vision* is a view of what the world will look like when the change becomes the new normal. It's an essential first step that this is created as a group – to craft a vision that is ambitious and compelling and serves as the foundation for everything which happens after this point. It provides purpose and the "why" for leaders and everyone else as well. Without a vision, there is no clear aim and transformation is likely to fail.

Why It Matters?

With a Vision:

- We give people a picture of the destination – where we will get to if we are successful
- We energize people around what is possible and what "could be"
- We give people a reason to make the journey – that the short-term challenges we face will be worth it for the long-term gain
- We talk specifically to those people whose preferred communication style is all about the bigger picture and where this takes us

- We have a clear focus on the wider change story and ensure that the change is communicated in a synchronized way throughout, for example, a bigger organization

Without a Vision:

- How will we know if we've been successful?
- People might know what we are doing, but will not understand why
- We fail to inspire people with possibilities
- We could lose people on the journey as the difficulties don't seem worth it
- We can talk about what is happening but cannot define what good will look like
- There will be different understandings of the change as there is not one overall north star for the change

Is there an existing vision that you can use?

Leaders have a critical role to play in sharing the vision with their teams. It forms a key part of the change setting the north star for the organization and should continually be communicated throughout the change process.

When getting ready for a change, and before your teams have been communicated to, ask yourself the following question:

> **Do we have a strong compelling change vision ready? If yes, then that's good news** – there is an aligned vision for the change that, hopefully, all leaders will be able to use and share with their teams.

On a practical level you should:

Take this vision and consider how it applies directly to your team – how can you connect your day-to-day work to the outcome?

Use it as part of the change story[2] you need to build for communicating and engaging with your team. Ensure, whenever you communicate to your team, that you connect to this vision. Finally, make sure that you have commitment from sponsors and the steering committee or any other group you need support from.

If you do not have a change vision then…

- Explore with, among others, the core team and leaders delivering the change, what would the best approach be. What would a change vision workshop look like?
- Be sure to explain the importance of the change vision and involve key stakeholders and sponsors of the change in the creation of the vision – to create ownership of the change.
- You can use this workshop approach to create a vision for the change.

How to Bring It into Action?

Inspirational Facilitation Overview for a Change Vision Workshop

Introduction	**Key point: To introduce the topic and ensure participants understand why they're here today.**
	Welcome everyone to the workshop. Do introductions if necessary. Introduce the objectives and ensure that participants understand the purpose of the workshop.
	We're here today to create a vision for the change/transformation – a bold, inspiring statement that gives us all a sense of purpose and guides us on the journey.
	The outcome will be:
	• *A rich, compelling description of what the change should achieve that can be used as an "anchor" throughout the journey*
	• *Clarity on why we're making this change, expressed in powerful language*
	• *Alignment on some aspects of what the change will mean*
	Points to Explain:
	• This session is intended to create a vision for our change
	• As leaders, we need to agree on why we're doing it before we talk to the wider audience
	• Getting people to accept change is one thing; encouraging them to actively believe in it and pursue it is quite another
	This is a creative session, please don't feel the need to get the answer perfect from the beginning – be comfortable sharing your thoughts.
	Ask: What do you think we mean by a vision? Does anyone have a good example they'd like to share?
	Share examples of compelling visions. Incorporate any strong change visions from elsewhere as well – either add them to the slide as you discuss/get examples from the group or think it over beforehand.
	Explain that a good vision paints a picture of the future and incorporates the purpose of the change. Show that these range from detailed (e.g., The LEGO Group example below) to purely visionary, but all of them are bold, ambitious, and inspiring. They are also simple and easily understood rather than being complex and full of jargon.
	LEGO Vision Example:
	Inventing the future of play. "We want to pioneer new ways of playing, play materials and the business models of play – leveraging globalization and digitalization... it is not just about products, it is about realizing the human possibility."
	"To inspire and develop the builders of tomorrow."

Paint a picture of the future	**Key point: To explore aspects of the change as inspiration for creating the vision.** Ask them to imagine they are in the future, once the change has worked. This is an optimistic exercise. Allow them 30 minutes to fill in answers to the questions about what will change. **Relationships:** What has changed? What new relationships have formed? **Organization:** How has the structure changed? What has been gained/lost? **Ways of working:** How are people working differently? Do we have different processes or systems? **Culture and behaviors:** How has the culture changed? Are people behaving differently? **Skills and capabilities:** What new skills have emerged? **Performance:** How have different teams, units, or the whole business changed in terms of performance? **Customer:** How has the customer been impacted? **Mindset and emotions:** How are people feeling? What do they believe? Keep up the pace – this is not intended as a full impact analysis. Once complete, ask each group to share what they captured.
Craft the statement	**Key point: To run through several iterations of the statement, improving it as they go and eventually landing on something people can get behind.** Explain that it's time to craft a vision statement. Give each person 5 minutes to write their statement alone. The only rules: • No more than 35 words • Speak as you write • Be bold! Then put people into pairs and tell them to read their statements to one another. Together they should combine the best elements of each and develop a new iteration.
Make it even better	Ask them to use these principles, in their pairs, and create their last version • Do you say what you will do? Does it give clear direction? • Use self-disclosure and personal reflection • Relate the story to your personal experience • Avoid using generic phrases and being too broad • Could it create confusion? Avoid complex language

	Ask them to write their statement large on a piece of paper for sharing. Each pair then reads out their statement to the rest of the room. Facilitate a brief discussion around which elements and phrases from each shared vision the group thinks are the most critical and powerful – write these up on a flipchart. **Explain** that a small group will work together after the session to bring together and refine these key elements. They will spend time polishing the final version of the words and will ensure it reflects the groups' input today. Promise a specific delivery date as soon as possible.
Into action	**Key point: To set actions for how this vision will be shared with the rest of the organization.** Explain that a vision is only useful if it's widely understood. Once we have the final version, how should we share it with everyone else? Run a short brainstorming session to consider where and how the vision can be shared.
	Provide a couple of examples to help start the discussion if needed: • Animation or video • Email • Yammer • Create a rich picture • Face-to-face meetings/townhalls and conversations • Desk drops or physical materials Everyone has a duty to share this vision with people around the business (once it's polished). Each person then promises to take away an action that they share with the room. They should name a person (or people) that they will explain the vision to – and when they plan to do it. Write down everyone's commitment on a flipchart or whiteboard. Thank everyone for their participation as you close the session
Post-session **Tidy and craft action**	A small group take away the final preferred statement and, with as little editing as possible, craft the words for the final edit. Aim to do this as soon as possible after the session and send to attendees swiftly afterwards, along with a reminder of who they committed to share it with and when. You could also use expertise from communications teams to help with the final wording. When crafting the statement, make sure the vision is simple, engaging, and free of jargon – you should be able to share it with someone who doesn't work in your company and they should be able to understand it. When you feed the statement back to the larger group, ask them to use these three criteria to judge whether you have achieved your aim. Note: The vision may change during the course of the Change Journey, so don't be too defensive about it. However, do not alter it unless circumstances strongly suggest it is no longer fit for the purpose.

TOP TIPS – GETTING READY

1. To create the change vision is an essential first step and works as the foundation for everything which happens after this point. Without a vision, there is not a clear aim and the change is likely to fail.
2. Aim to inspire, be descriptive and specific. Convey a strong idea and include the long-term purpose.
3. A strong vision statement will not only help others understand the need for change but inspire them to get behind it with everything they have.
4. Don't use overly generic phrases, be too broad, use complex language, or lack direction.

SIGNS YOU'RE READY TO MOVE FORWARD...

■ You have a group of change leaders aligned and positive about the ambition to change
■ You have an understanding of the status quo at a business and human (behavioral) level
■ You have instilled trust in stakeholders

CASE STUDY: THE SPEED TO MARKET TRANSFORMATION

The change vision showed the way and built belief during the period of time when the program was losing focus and attention

By Palle Ditlevsen, Sr. Business Manager

CONTEXT OF THE SPEED TO MARKET TRANSFORMATION

The Speed to Market Program was a transformation initiative that was defined based on internal research performed during a difficult period when sales declined, particularly in the American market. The research concluded that the LEGO Group needed to reinvent ways to ensure LEGO products were new, relevant, and cool – to boost newness in the eyes of kids.

The aim was to improve business formulas to meet rapidly changing demands and expectations among kids, parents, and shoppers. There was a need to be more adaptive to rapid changes in the marketplace. The adaptiveness also included the operating model and ensuring that the operating model was continuously fit for purpose.

One way to accomplish this was by the launch of the Speed to Market initiative with the aim of accelerating and shortening the path from Opportunity to Launch – this was considered as a vehicle for change. *The direction was set; it should be a transformation – big enough to make a radical step change.*

Palle Ditlevsen, Sr. Business Manager, explains:

> We were briefed to rethink our ways of working, optimizing across processes with radical improvements across business areas in development, manufacturing and marketing groups, in a way that we had never been allowed to do before. And we only had 3 months to create the first results through a pilot initiative.
>
> The approach was to test and learn new ways of working and we worked really hard to create results fast, and the idea was to test and learn first, and then figure out how to do it in a more systematic way. There was huge interest and attention around the initiative, from both leaders and subject matter experts, being willing and eager to be part of and to engage in the initiative. Based on learnings from the pilot we pitched a storyline on how we systematically could enable speed across the entire value chain to our senior leadership stakeholders and suddenly this storyline was presented by our CEO at the LEGO Townhall for all LEGO employees, and at a later point a LEGO Web article was shared with one of the senior leaders to explain more details on the journey of Speed to Market. That created additionally a lot of attention and progression.

However, it became clear that the transformation efforts would take much longer than the senior leadership attention would last. New priorities to make a turnaround and get back on track in the company took the full focus. In the initial program projects, internal consultants helped product development teams identify and implement new ways of working across a broad range of functional organizations involved. Victory was declared when the winning formula systematically enabled greater speed and then the consultants were moved into other areas to repeat and scale their efforts there.

> As it turned out, though, the victory was declared too early. Changing behaviors and ways of working required bigger efforts and more attention from the departments involved.[3] There is no doubt that the vision and the north star was there from the very beginning, but was much more latent and implicit in the storylines that came from senior leaders. Based on the burning platform of declining sales in the US market, everybody bought into the why of this important initiative. In order to regain focus and progression, the program team was expanded with increased change management capabilities. And as a part of this, a vision was formulated to be more explicit and deployed more systematically in the coming program streams.

So in this case, the change vision was not formulated and made explicit in the first wave of success. We could see that there was still a strong need for leaders and the areas involved in the transformation to build and connect to the overall vision. Without that, the loss of focus led to confusion as the changes in working patterns and behaviors proceeded without this clear vision.

> Ditlevsen explains:

> We had some great content to dig into, both from the Townhall and the LEGO Web article, and additionally there were important findings from the research work that had been done. Based on this, we brought together a small team consisting of the Program Manager, the Change Partner, the Communication Partner and a business partner, and based on the available content we drafted the change vision. We included elements like ways of working, behaviors, performance and consumers.

We were very focused on having both an external perspective and an internal perspective included in the vision, and making sure that it was very clear who we are doing it for. We ended up with this vision statement:

> *Today, kids live in a rapidly changing world. To keep delivering hot and appealing play experiences in this environment, we need to make decisions closer to when the products hit the shelves. This requires us to shorten the time it takes to develop, make and sell our products.*

The vision was presented to the Steering Group and signed off. Additionally, it was used in engagement sessions, training sessions, and not the least with all involved leaders creating their change stories based on this overall direction to ensure consistency. It enabled everyone to build belief in the communication and engagement activities taken by the different teams which created strong synergy and commitment across the different business areas in Development, Manufacturing, and Sales.

Reconnecting to the overall vision and ambition, getting the right capabilities, and focusing on the program team along with strong collaboration with people leaders from impacted teams, the program got back on track and succeeded with the defined objectives of reducing lead times from Opportunity to Launch.

Notes

1. Mahatma Gandhi, 1913.
2. More inspiration on Change Story Workshop in Chapter 5.
3. You can read more about how we managed to anchor the Speed to Market transformation in Chapter 8.

CHAPTER 5

MOMENT 2 – UNDERSTANDING THE CHANGE

What Is It?

This is the moment when leaders have already agreed on the high-level purpose of change, but it's now time to dive into the specifics and build a plan for the right options to deliver on that purpose. Additionally, this is also the moment where you get more understanding of the impact the change will have on people and prepare yourself to engage with the impacted teams.

Possible signs that indicate we need people to understand the change

- When asked what the change will look like, leaders talk in soundbites and broad statements
- Everyone can explain the rationale, but the details aren't there yet
- Leaders talk about the people affected by the change in general or unrealistically pessimistic/optimistic terms
- It's not yet clear what real roles people are playing in the change

How people are feeling

- "I'm *thrilled*! We're going to transform the whole company overnight!"
- "I'm *energized* – Finally, we're doing things differently. When can I start?"
- "I'm *intrigued* – It could be good, but I don't know enough to judge yet."
- "I'm *overwhelmed* – It's going to be really difficult."
- "I'm *suspicious* – What's really going on that they're not telling us?"
- "I'm *scared*... Will my role change? Will I lose my job?"

 DOI: 10.4324/9781003243113-5

Why It Matters?

If we get this moment right, we'll get:

- Buy-in and commitment from key people and leaders
- A strong understanding of the impact and journey and what's required to make it a success
- Emerging catalysts

If we don't get it right:

- Passive resistance and cynics
- Panic which can destabilize daily operations
- A design that works on paper but not in practice
- False expectations

WHERE AND HOW CAN YOU HAVE THE BIGGEST IMPACT?

For relevant stakeholders and people or teams being impacted, understanding the change is critically important to succeed in a good change journey. Having a strong understanding of the change will also enable you to engage others with the change and explain to others what the change will mean in relation to their daily work. This is often one of the areas with the least investment, but being able to explain the change in specific terms and how this will impact the way people are working today will make people feel more confident and comfortable with the change. There are many different tactics on how to help people understand the change better – here, you can find five different experiences and tools that you can bring into play.

Where	How
A critical factor in successful change is identifying and managing all stakeholders that have either influence or an interest in the change.	**Understanding Your Stakeholders page 46**
Help make the change feel real and understand the impact and trade-offs – and avoid surprises.	**Change Impact Analysis page 48**
Prepare yourself to engage with your team in an authentic way and make people feel listened to. Be able to facilitate a clear, sufficiently detailed change story.	**Change Story workshop page 54**
Get insights into how change ready your team is – and improve change readiness for leaders and their teams.	**Change Readiness Assessment page 66**
All changes are about people. As a leader, it is your job to lead change from the top. Your catalysts should be on hand, helping lead change from the ground.	**Catch the Catalyst page 72**

Understanding Your Stakeholders

What Is It?

A critical factor in successful change is identifying and managing all stakeholders that have either influence or an interest in what you are trying to achieve. The purpose of this tool is to help you map all of these key stakeholders and define a plan for keeping them engaged.

Who Is a Stakeholder?

A stakeholder is either an individual, group, or organization that is impacted by the outcome of a change. They have an interest in the success of the change and can be within or outside the organization. Stakeholders can have a positive or negative influence on the change. The change will usually have a range of stakeholders with different levels of influence and interest with regard to the outcome of the change.

Why It Matters?

If you can successfully manage the full stakeholder ecosystem of the change, you will be better equipped for success. Failure to manage stakeholders is one of the biggest failure points of most change efforts – if it is done poorly or not at all. Your most powerful stakeholders can help to drive and shape the change, gain resources, prioritize demands, and remove obstacles. They also have the potential to derail you if they are not handled correctly.

How to Bring It into Action?

You should ideally start mapping and managing stakeholders at the very beginning of the change, then evolve and revisit the mapping throughout the change. It should exist as a dynamic, live map/document which captures the temperature of the stakeholder landscape at any given moment.

The guidance on the next page sets out how to define and build your stakeholder map. In simple terms, there are three key steps:

1. **Map**: Identify all of the stakeholders for the change and consider, for example, their strengths, weaknesses, daily challenges, motivations, attitudes toward the change, and the biggest questions they have about the change. Additionally, define their level of *Influence* and *Interest* in the change outcome:
   INFLUENCE: The level of influence the stakeholder has over the direction and success of the change.
   INTEREST: The level of interest the stakeholder has in the progress and outcome of the change.
   Mapping against these two dimensions creates four stakeholder categories, all of which require different levels of engagement and treatment:
   - High influence, high interest: Partner and closely manage throughout the full program cycle.
   - High influence, low interest: Keep fully informed and satisfied.
   - Low influence, high interest: Anticipate needs and keep informed regularly.
   - Low influence, low interest: Monitor and keep updates/contact minimal.

It can simplify the process if you map out stakeholder groups, and only individuals where relevant.

2. **Plan**: Define the engagement plan, actions, and owners for each of the stakeholder groups.
3. **Manage**: Continually revisit and refresh the mapping to ensure all stakeholders are engaged and issues are dealt with.

It is worth noting that the Change Impact Analysis (Figure 5.5) and the Stakeholder Mapping (Figure 5.1) and Communications & Engagement Plan (Figure 5.2) also described in this chapter are tools that should be seen as supplementary to each other. As each initiative will be different, depending on the nature and complexity, you will need to decide on a case-by-case basis the best approach where it makes sense to combine versus separate these tools.

There are various ways in which these tools can be brought to life and developed in workshops and in interaction with people to know the business and understand the change.

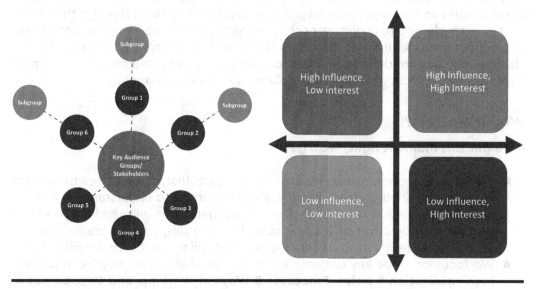

Figure 5.1 Mapping out your stakeholders.

Business Process	Activity	Lead
Leadership Seminar	Seminar	N/A
MVC	Portfolio Presentation	N/A
Stakeholder(s)	**Activity**	**Lead**
PG Leads	Channel engagement sessions	Steen
PG Marketing Managers	Channel engagement sessions	Steen
BMIP	TBC	TBC
Regional Marketing Teams	TBC	TBC
Regional Sales & Channel Teams	TBC	TBC
MG Heads	TBC	TBC
BU GMs	TBC	TBC
BU Marketing Teams	TBC	TBC
BU Sales & Channel Teams	TBC	TBC
Ops Sub-LTs	TBC	TBC

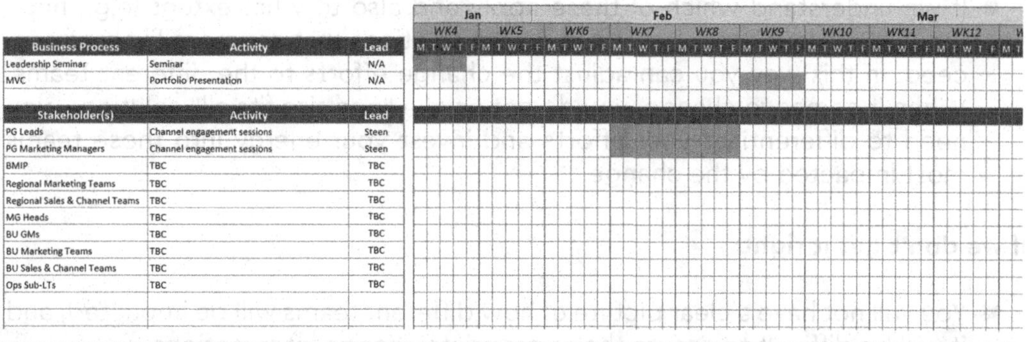

Figure 5.2 Communication & engagement plan (example).

Change Impact Analysis

What Is It?

The Change Impact Analysis (CIA) is a critical step to identify potential consequences of the change and to get accurate understanding of the implications of those consequences. Skipping the CIA does not change the size of the task, but it will turn into an unpredictable and unforeseeable matter. So performing the analysis helps to ensure that you involve the impacted people and stakeholders and that you are able to create an appropriate journey that is adjusted to the impact the change will have on them. This will include identifying how key audience groups will be impacted and what needs to be done to help them reach the objectives of the future state.

The process around the tool is iterative and the content should be revisited, when necessary, throughout the transformation. Therefore, it is natural to begin with a simple analysis of current and future state processes, organization, roles, etc., followed by collection of more details via workshops and/or interviews. It is very common that additional changes and more impacted teams will surface in the dialogues and as new knowledge comes up while working through the analysis. For example, you may discover other teams or individuals being impacted that you did not consider upfront. Based on the identified changes and impact levels, change activities are defined in order to manage the identified changes and mitigate risks through capability building plans/competency mapping.

Why It Matters?

If we get this moment right, we'll get:

- Within a change initiative, it's usually the case that different teams will be impacted in different ways. It is therefore important to understand, at a more granular level, exactly how each part of the organization will need to change to support the objectives of your initiative. In doing this, you can create relevant change activities for each audience group that will support their specific needs.
- We focus on three key dimensions of change that teams may be impacted by: **Organization & Roles, Processes & Ways of Working, and Capabilities & Skills**. By taking into account these three dimensions, you analyze from various angles, minimizing surprises and impacts that you may not have considered.
- If we understand which of these apply and also to what extent (e.g., high, medium, or low impact), we can create solutions that are more likely to succeed. In this way you can adjust the change efforts to the different teams. When it comes to change, you do not have a "one size fits all" solution – you need to differentiate your efforts and invest your energy into those teams most impacted by the change.

If we don't get it right:

- You will not have a clear picture of how different teams will be impacted, and it will be difficult to ensure the appropriate change interventions.

- There might be surprises and obstacles you have not thought of and that could have been avoided.
- There might be teams that are being impacted that you have not engaged with nor included in the change journey, resulting in people feeling excluded or not being part of the change.

How to Bring It into Action?

You can conduct the CIA at different times during the change and you should consider it as an iterative process. However, it is a natural point of time to start this initiative when you are working on understanding the change. You can start by identifying key changes at a high level. In addition, it is useful to describe the "From–To" picture of the key changes. By doing so, it's easier for people to understand and relate to as it is linked to how things are today. Additionally, it can be very useful to take as a starting point, for example, the team level, with focus on how a specific team will be impacted by the change. Here is an example of a "From–To" picture as part of the CIA (Figure 5.3).

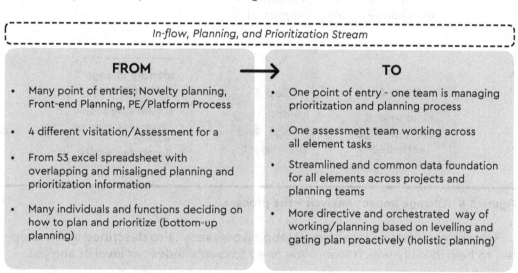

Figure 5.3   Examples of "From–To" overview.

The best time to conduct a change impact analysis is when there is a solid overview of the future state (approx. 80% of the future state). This will be the point of time where you can combine the knowledge of the existing context and also have sufficient knowledge about the future state. This means that people can relate to both worlds and the change impact will thereby be clearer. The CIA is also a great dialogue tool and, whether or not individuals/teams/leaders have been involved in the change so far, it is a great time and opportunity to get people on board to involve them and create a common understanding of the change impact.

Creating the analysis is not a theoretical desk exercise; it can only be done with people who know the existing business, organization, and ways of working. Additionally, you need to include people who have been a part of defining the future state (processes, roles, etc.). This is a great opportunity to bring together people who know the existing and the future state to map out the change impact and what key considerations/actions need to be taken to ensure a smooth and engaging change journey. The value this process creates is a common under-standing of the change and what is needed to make the change successful. And, additionally, also being able to communicate what the change is about.

Finally, it's important to emphasize that the CIA can be done both for bigger transformation initiatives and also in smaller changes. It is a fully adaptable tool depending on the specific context.

The following guide (Figure 5.4) outlines the specific steps of how to use the tool. Once you have created the overview, you will need to use the actions you have identified as the backbone of your change plan – i.e., what you are actually going to do to manage the impact on the target audience(s).

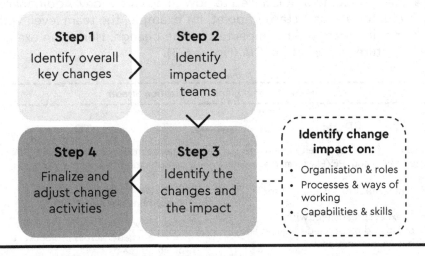

Figure 5.4   Change Impact Analysis – the process.

Use the completed Stakeholder Mapping overview (also described in this chapter) to help identify which teams you need to create a deeper level of analysis.

Step 1: Identify overall key changes

■ First, map out the key changes.

Step 2: Identify impacted teams

■ The next step is to identify which teams or areas will be impacted by the change.
■ If you have completed the Stakeholder Mapping tool, then use this as your starting point, but not all stakeholders require a detailed impact analysis. Focus on the areas being most impacted.

The key criteria for deciding who needs to be part of the analysis could be:

■ Which teams will be impacted by how they work today?
■ Which teams will be organizationally impacted by the change?

This might be only one team, or it could be many groups across different parts of the organization. You will need to use your criteria to decide exactly who needs to be included. To make sure you get this right, it is usually best to work with the project team and business leads to ensure that you have captured all of the relevant teams.

Step 3: Identify the changes and the impact based on facilitating questions

■ Once you have the key changes and the impacted teams identified, you can complete the analysis. Specific guidance on how to do this is in the tool but, in general, you are seeking to map out the change impact as high, medium, or low against the following three dimensions – here are facilitation questions that you can use in, for example, a workshop or interview.

1. **Organization and roles**
   - Are there changes to roles and responsibilities? What are the changes?
   - Will there be changes in interfaces, for example, who will work together with who? What are the changes?
   - Do the changes require different and/or new functions/teams in the organization?
2. **Processes and ways of working**
   - Are there changes to the core processes? What are the changes?
   - Will the local business environment challenge the implementation of the process? What will they challenge?
   - Is there commitment to process standardization?
   - Do the changes require new behaviors to complete the daily tasks? What are the changes?
   - Do the changes require new attitudes to complete the daily tasks? What are the changes?
3. **Capabilities and skills**
   - Are there new skills and knowledge to be acquired? What are the new skills needed to solve the tasks and follow the processes?
   - Are the new skills needed in multiple roles?

There are different ways of creating the analysis depending on who is available and also who you can speak to if the change is confidential at this stage. This will enable a 360-degree perspective of the change.

The easiest flow is to first create an overview using a deep-dive workshop with, e.g., the project team and business leads/specialists. The workshop can be from half a day to a full day, if possible. It is key to get strong business specialists on board for this task, people who know the business and the ways of working and, at the same time, individuals who can explain what they do. It is one thing to do a job and execute it on a daily basis, but a completely different thing to explain what you are doing. Below is a template of what the overview could look like (Figure 5.5).

Team	Role	Key changes and considerations	Organization & roles	Processes & Ways of Working	Capabilities & skills
Marketing	Digital Marketing	• Greater specialization of activities*, with creative/analytics, performance-focused search, and marketing activities shifting to regional teams • Cross-functional coordination with local and regional activities, Marketing teams, including regional execution	Green		
			Amber	Red	

Figure 5.5 Change Impact Analysis – overview.

There are other ways of collecting data for the CIA. It could be mapped out by interviewing different stakeholders and business specialists. There are many advantages of doing the analysis in the workshop as a team to create a common understanding of the change. However, there may be time or resource constraints that won't allow for such a workshop, and here, an alternative could be doing interviews with individuals or a few people at a time.

Creating a visual heatmap, as in Figure 5.5, is a powerful and easy-to-understand way to indicate to what extent the teams will be impacted by the change.

Below is an example of the change impact categorization (Figure 5.6) which helps ensure that you have a consistent way to categorize the nature of the change

	LOW (Green)	MEDIUM (Amber)	HIGH (Red)
	People impacted only need to make minor (or no) changes to their daily work as a result of the initiative	There will be multiple changes to the way people do their job as a result of this initiative	The initiative will result in a fundamental change to the way people do their job
Organization & Roles	- Zero or minor changes to where work is performed - Zero or minor changes to working relationships - Zero or minor changes to roles, accountabilities, mandates	- Notable changes to where work is performed - Adjustment to working relationships required to perform role - Changes to roles, accountabilities, mandates. Introduction of new roles	- Large-scale changes to where work is performed - Total changes to working relationships - Full re-organisation of roles, accountabilities, mandates
Processes & Ways of Working	- Zero or minor adjustments to existing ways of working - Zero or minor adjustments to existing processes or systems	- New platform or significant adjustment to existing platform - Significant adjustments to existing process	- Total change to technology platforms used - Introduction of completely new processes for core role requirements
Capabilities & Skills	- Zero or minor skills/knowledge training required - Required capabilities already present	- Training, coaching and support required for new skills/knowledge - New capabilities required in some roles	- Extensive training required to develop new knowledge/skills - Multiple new capabilities required/ new core capability required

Figure 5.6 Change Impact Categorization.

by using Red (high-level impact), Yellow (medium level of impact), or Green (no or minor level of impact).

The project team will get you a strong baseline, but you should ideally look to validate your analysis with people that represent or can speak on behalf of the different teams in the impact analysis. This can be done by connecting with a couple of team members from the impacted teams and walking with them through the analysis, adding or refining the content based on their comments and input.

Additionally, if you are analyzing different elements from a wider context, it is important to connect all the dots and ensure that the data are aligned and not contradictory.

During this process, it is vital to capture the "nuances" or hidden challenges that the project team might not be aware of – for example, a certain team having a long history and pride in a certain process that will present a very specific behavioral challenge.

Step 4: Finalize and adjust the change activities

- When you are confident the analysis is covering the relevant areas and the relevant key changes, then you can extract and finalize agreed-upon change management activities and use this as the basis for your planning and contracting on the project.
- You will need to set out these activities against timelines and begin the process of agreeing with the project team (or steering committee) on what can realistically be achieved, where ownership lies, what resources are required, and how much time will be needed with the business/impacted teams.
- Revisit the change activities you have planned and adjust the activities so they are matching the levels of the change impact. Ensure that you will be investing time and effort in those teams or areas that are impacted the most.

Change Story Workshop

What Is It?

You have crafted your vision statement[1] and you have a good view of the change impact; now, it's time to bring it to life. It's important to think about what you want to achieve here. You've created a vision for what the future should look like, and now you want to convey this message in a way that will build belief in the change. Familiarize yourself with the vision statement and the change impact, and learn how to communicate this message effectively through storytelling.

One story or many? What are you trying to achieve? It's possible to create one common story each leader can tell, but there's a risk of losing the authentic connection that each individual has with what they're saying – and thereby failing to connect with their audience. Use the Change Story Workshop to agree on the common, essential ingredients of the story, but then let individuals find their own spin on it – their own language, metaphors, examples, and personal interpretations. This will also make the story more relevant for the teams the leaders are communicating to. They can always be inspired by each other, but ultimately you can only build belief when you *own* what you're saying.

Additionally, it can be quite fruitful to look at your preferred communication style and how this impacts your team. You should also create some awareness of your strengths versus potential blind spots.

Why It Matters?

Connecting with your team through times of change is a critical success factor. It's important to understand what good communication looks like and the tools and techniques you can use to better engage and communicate. More importantly, you must also work through how you can do this authentically – in a way you're comfortable and confident with so it feels natural for you and you are perceived to be authentic. You should see communication and engagement as critical levers in driving successful change.

These should be natural factors, but it's very common to see changes fail or achieve limited results due to lack of information or limited opportunities to connect with and understand people. "There was just too much communication and information throughout this change" is something you never hear. There are some critical elements of what good looks like, but for now, keep in mind that we deliberately referred to this as communications AND engagement rather than just communication. And this is relevant for both smaller changes and bigger transformations.

Communicating and engaging with, for example, your team will be more natural for you if you are aware of your own communication style – and also consider the styles of the people you are communicating with.

Storytelling

Leaders driving change need to make sense of the journey and practice how they articulate it to their teams and colleagues. They need to feel ownership of the specifics – what will be impacted by the change and why. They also need a narrative to explain the rationale and the coming journey. Stories are the most powerful tool at their disposal as they're intuitive, persuasive, and engaging.

Delivering a message and building belief in a message are two different things. For people to get behind and engaged with the change, the message needs to be delivered in an authentic and compelling way, a way that resonates with the audience.

People have evolved to think in a narrative way. Well-told stories stick with us, making them more powerful influencing tools than rational argument. Compelling change stories can build emotional connections, also known as neural coupling, where a story activates the neurons in a listener's brain allowing them to experience the story as their own.

A well-told story engages multiple areas of the brain, including the motor cortex, sensory cortex, and frontal cortex, making stories easier to digest and remember than other forms of information. Listeners will experience similar brain activity with each other as well as the speaker, creating empathy and a shared experience in an easily digestible way. Listening to an emotional story releases dopamine – activating the brain's reward and pleasure centers. This can make a well-told story highly inspiring.

Most importantly, stories are the most powerful way to communicate the WHY behind a change, rather than just the WHAT.

How to Bring It into Action?

Inspirational Facilitation Overview for a Change Story Workshop

Introduction	**Key point: To introduce the day and ensure participants understand the purpose of the workshop.** Welcome everyone to the workshop. Do introductions if necessary and maybe an icebreaker. Introduce that day and ensure participants understand the purpose of the workshop. Explain outcome of the session: • More self-awareness of their communication and engagement styles – and dialogues on how they, as a team leaders, can support each other based on their different styles • Structured and practiced early versions of each leader's change story • Ensure they can talk about these stories in humane, authentic, and credible language • Agreed practical use of their personal story back in the workplace Inspirational agenda: 1. **Introduction to Communication & Engagement** – what does good look like and what types of things should I be doing? 2. **Understanding Your Communication Style** – what is my style and the associated strengths/blind spots? 3. **Crafting Your Change Story** – how do I talk about the change with my team? 4. **Into Action** – what can I do back in the office to implement some of these ideas?

Communication and engagement	**Key point: To get a view of what good looks like as to communication and engagement when leading successful change.**
	Explain that communication and engagement are critical levers in driving successful change. And that these should be natural factors, but it's very common to see changes fail or achieve limited results due to lack of information or limited opportunities to connect with and understand people.
	Explain that we are going to step through some of the critical elements of what good looks like – and keep in mind that we're deliberately referring to this as communication AND engagement rather than just communication.
	Ask the audience the question: *Can you give examples of the types of communication and engagement activities that should be in place for people during times of change?*
	Gather responses in plenum or the online chat, or on a flipchart.
	If people are struggling, provide prompts such as:
	What channels or methods (e.g., email, calls) could be used?
	Who would be responsible for communication and what might they do?
	Get some initial ideas and baseline the level of understanding around what is possible within the room – keep it tight and focused.
	e.g., Active Listening
	Being Present
	Role Modelling
The role of communication and engagement	Show the overview of the role of communication and engagement (Figure 5.7 on page 63), and refer back to the examples that were called out by the leaders in the previous exercise – and walk them through each of the different elements in the model.
	Ownership: When leaders at all levels take ownership of talking to their people about the change, start dialogues with them and seek to understand their views. They will be hungry for more information, opportunities to discuss the change, and to share their views.
	Direction: However, we need to see this as a two-way street – how are we creating a two-way dialogue so we're talking to people but also LISTENING. E.g., setting aside time on team calls just to discuss how people are feeling, their views, their questions, etc.
	Channel: For example, a monthly email or call is great as a starting point, but greater value will be driven through a multi-channel approach. Consider mechanisms like email updates, team calls, 1:1 check-ins, drop-in sessions, Yammer, feedback channels, etc.
	Plans: Are you adapting to questions and needs coming up? In an ideal world you will have some way of getting feedback from your people and then adjusting your engagement approach accordingly.

	Source: This is related to ownership – think through the type of communication you usually receive during change and it's very top-down – i.e., a cascade of what is happening and when, from a central perspective. However, when the time is right, find a way to create a richer picture through stories.
	Focus: People can spot a fake very easily. This is about not sugar-coating it. If we only focus on positive news and try to bury problems/bad news, then this will disengage people. A mix of good and bad news is most effective for driving belief in and support for change.
	Wrap-up: We don't expect you to remember all of this, and we'll come back to the specific actions later on in the session – refer back and consider what you can do differently in light of this information.
Communication styles	**Key point: To understand different communication styles and to become aware of your own style.**
	In case you are conducting the workshop face-to-face you can do this very interactively and use the room you are in.
	Explain that the next part is going to be a bit more interactive:
	<ul><li>Ask people to stand up.</li><li>The purpose of this session will be to look at your preferred communication style and how this impacts your team: what are your strengths vs. potential blind spots.</li><li>It's not an exact science – with more time we'd normally baseline this with pre-work and questionnaires.</li></ul>
	This is a vastly complex picture but to keep things simple, there are four key preferences when it comes to how we engage with information.
	Briefly summarize each quadrant/style (Figure 5.8 on page 63)
	Ask people to spend some time thinking through which one is most like them/their strongest preference.
	Clearly identify the four corners of the room as yellow, blue, green, or red. (Mirror the slide, e.g., front left corner of the room is yellow and the front right corner is blue, etc.) so, e.g., Reason and Emotion are in opposite corners
	1. Ask people to move to the corner that they have decided represents their strongest preference. It's not an exact science!! You will be a mix of these, just think about where your *strongest* tendencies are – there's no perfect match.
	2. If you are really struggling, think about which LEAST represents you, then go to the opposite corner.

	Look at the spread and note that with most teams (as there should be in the room) there are people in all four corners.
	Now, pick on one corner and ask them to describe the communications style of the OPPOSITE corner (e.g., for the reds, describe a change in a "yellow" way). Then ask them whether this was interesting for them/ gave them what they need.
	The room may need some prompting so encourage them to think about how they would feel on a normal day in the office if they heard that message – what would they be thinking? Would they want more of something or less?
	The idea is that they find the messaging disengaging and prefer/need different information.
	Repeat this exercise for all corners so everyone can get a sense of how it feels to receive communications in a style that they don't identify with.
	Some in the room might find this quite difficult in terms of placing themselves and really seeing the differentiation. It's important to keep in mind that these are preferences and some people have stronger preferences than others.
	The point of the exercise isn't to be perfect, it's to demonstrate the point that there are varying communication needs in their teams and that their style could have an impact on how well messages land.
	In case you are not physically together, the exercise can be used as a dialogue tool and you can pair up people to break them out in smaller teams and bring the following questions into play: **Dialogue questions:** What is your strongest preference? How do I really bring my strengths to the table during change? What actions can I take to close the blind spots? Can I use other styles? **breakout:** • 5 min: Each to reflect on their own preferred style. • 25 min: Each to share their preferred style with their group + group to discuss the questions above. Use examples. **plenum:** • Each group shares their takeaways and we discuss in plenum how we can use these insights in day-to-day collaboration using virtual whiteboards. Play back and align the plenary input to the visual (Figure 5.9 on page 64).

Why stories?	**Key point: To understand the power of stories in communicating change.**
	Explain that we have already talked about different elements of how you might communicate and engage with your teams. Now we're going to invest some time in how to structure your messages for maximum effect. Talking about a "change story" is probably something you've heard about – but what does this actually look like?
	We won't go into it now, but there is a huge amount of science telling us that the most effective method of communicating information is storytelling.
	• **Historical channel:** Until very recently we didn't write a lot down so we were dependent on stories to transmit and retain key information and knowledge.
	• **Neural activation:** Stories activate neural circuits in a way that maximizes retention and releases dopamine (pleasure and reward) which drives an emotional response to stories.
	• **Naturally organized:** Much easier to understand than lists and artificially organized information.
	• **Shared experience:** Create a shared experience and narrative that binds people – e.g., you will have college friends that can all recount the same stories in the same way and that drives group cohesion.
	• In summary – storytelling is a natural, hugely effective channel for engaging and communicating.
Telling your story 1	**Key point: To create a storyline without a structure.**
	Explain that now we are going to deliberately put you under a little bit of pressure. If participants challenge the level of ambiguity in the specific case for change, encourage them to just work with what they know as that is representative of reality right now. Just because they don't have all of the details, doesn't mean they won't have to engage with their teams.
	Set the context:
	You have just arrived at a site where a lot of your people work. It wasn't planned but a small townhall has been set up and you are expected to walk in and talk about the case for change.
	Brief on the following:
	• Spend just 5 minutes individually preparing your story/what you're going to say – what story will you tell about the change?
	• Get into pairs and share stories.
	• Give each other feedback – how did it come across? Was it clear? Are you missing anything?
	• Speakers – how did it feel trying to tell your story?
	Encourage to "just go with it – if you had to do this tomorrow, what would you do"? Remind them of the four different communication styles.
	Wrap up this exercise by hearing from a couple of groups about their experience, and explain that to tell the story in an effective and successful way, we have a tool that provides a structure and focus which maximizes understanding, engagement, and belief.

Telling your story 2	Key point: To introduce the change story structure and give them a chance to create their first version.
	Explain that this is like a book, we have "chapters" to make the story digestible.
	<ul><li>*Talk through the different elements (Figure 5.10 on page 64)*</li></ul>
	1. **Set the scene (context in which the story will play out)**
	Build a rich but simple picture of the background to your story. Describe the current situation and key conditions for change – e.g., what is/isn't working and why.
	2. **Explain the change (what is happening/changing)**
	What is the catalyst or incident that is driving the change? Be clear on the need. What is the rationale? What will the benefit be? Give details on why the change is appropriate. Why this direction and not another?
	3. **Make it personal (build a personal and emotional connection)**
	Begin with yourself – why do you believe this is right? What examples can you give? Move on to talk about us – why is this relevant to your audience? What do they care about and how can you connect with this? Give details of the benefit to the audience.
	4. **Summarize the journey (the actions that will follow and how it ends)**
	Be clear on key actions, next steps, and timelines. If something is unknown, be honest and open about this. Signpost where people can get involved and when they will hear something more. Give details of what support will be provided to your audience.
	5. **Describe the destination (where we will arrive at and how we'll look back)**
	Tie everything back to the vision for the change so people are clear on where we are trying to get to. Try to describe the destination in an engaging way – what will it look/feel like when they get there? Why will it be worth the journey?
	Big emphasis on authenticity: MAKE IT PERSONAL – a key element of humility and authenticity that we referenced earlier. How are you making this *yours* rather than just a copy & paste?
	Explain that you don't have to capture every single bullet point, but rather consider each of the five steps with the pointers provided to build your message. Individually, each person should use the story structure handout shared to create their own first draft story. Tell them to take inspiration from everything we've covered today, the activities, and the common foundations. Encourage them not to worry about incorporating everything, but to use their intuition and write it quickly – in 10 minutes or less.
	Explain that there is no right answer, providing they don't contradict the facts. Try to keep it brief – no more than 3 minutes to tell the story, so not too much detail.
	If you are working with a small group, ask for a volunteer to step up and tell their story to the room. If nobody is willing, get people to share their stories in pairs and give feedback. Then give them 10 minutes to make improvements based on this feedback (Figure 5.11 on page 65).

Authenticity	**Key point: To improve the credibility of the stories by asking participants to inject authenticity into them.**
	Explain that no matter how well we build our story, we need people to believe that we believe it. What organizations – and customers – really want and need during change is authentic leaders who aren't just reproducing the official management line or corporate nonsense. You need to be authentic... This matters, because people are expert at spotting when someone isn't being real, or consistent, or doesn't mean what they're saying. Change is a period of stress and skepticism – people need to trust their leaders more than ever. Being fake is exhausting and drives poor performance over time.
	Do what you say you will do: don't sugar-coat or make promises you can't keep, and follow up so people can see you're making progress. Use self-disclosure and personal reflection: share how you are feeling and what your reflections are on the change – don't just regurgitate a line you've memorized. Relate the story to your personal experience.
	Be consistent between people: make sure you don't change your story drastically between groups – some tweaking to suit your audience may make sense, but your themes should remain the same regardless of who you're talking to.
	Some examples to help you:
	• Emphasize the elements you personally find most exciting
	• Talk through your own journey to understanding the change – including what you didn't like or understand and how you feel now
	• Relate it to other experiences you've had
	Ask for any of their suggestions.
	Outputs: understanding and advice on how to make their change story both personal and credible.
	You now need to ask participants to *repeat the previous exercise (i.e., story build and sharing/feedback) but this time using the template you've just run through.*
	During feedback, encourage people to share whether this felt different.
	Bring people together in plenary at the end and prompt them to share their reflections – did the structure help? If so, how? Did you have more confidence as a speaker?

	Provide some of the following tips that you find most relevant: • Some simple guidance on HOW to build a story. • Keep it short – people will lose focus if it is too long. • Keep it simple – no jargon, figures, or acronyms. Would your neighbors understand it? • Keep it engaging – head & heart (ask for examples of great speeches – always an emotional element). • Set the tone – think about the context, the type of change, and how people will be feeling – set the tone accordingly. • Make it personal – drives emotional reaction and connection from audience… what's your connection/view? • Anchor – make sense in context of wider company ambition. During the next section you will ask them to think through how they start to use and share this. You learn a lot when you see yourself telling the story, so record it to make it as real as possible. And practice, so you are ready to go back and tell the story to your team.
Practice and refine	**Key point: We'll get better and more authentic at telling our stories by practicing them.** Assign pairs. Each person tells their story to their partner who then gives them fast feedback (on their template) on how it went: • Does it include the agreed-upon core components? • What made it compelling? • What made it authentic? • How could it be stronger? They then return the favor. Time permitting, give them a chance to try an improved version in another pair and repeat the feedback process. Finally, ask for volunteers to deliver their story to the room – and offer feedback that they can capture.
Into action	**Key point: To ensure leaders commit to using what they've developed together.** Show Figure 5.12 on page 65. Commit to action and summarize what you've covered in the session. Explain that now we need to agree on how to make practical use of their efforts. Recap the actions agreed upon in the morning after looking at the Impact Assessment. As individuals, ask each person to write down their actions. Tell them to think tangibly and with specifics, i.e., "I will use my story," isn't good enough. "At the team meeting on Tuesday I will talk through the change story with my team and ask for their thoughts," is better. Then ask each person to declare their actions to the room. Review what they say and consider if you think there may be gaps and where.

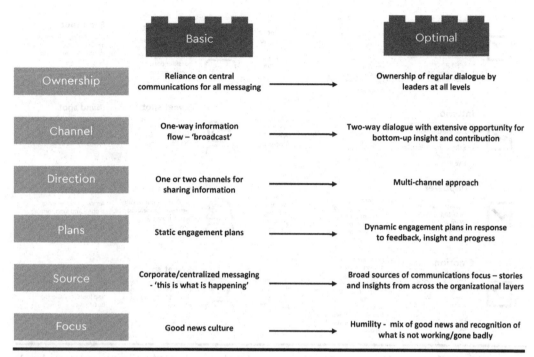

Figure 5.7   The role of communication & engagement.

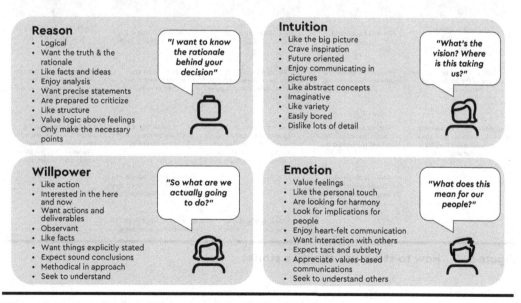

Figure 5.8   We all have different styles of engaging.

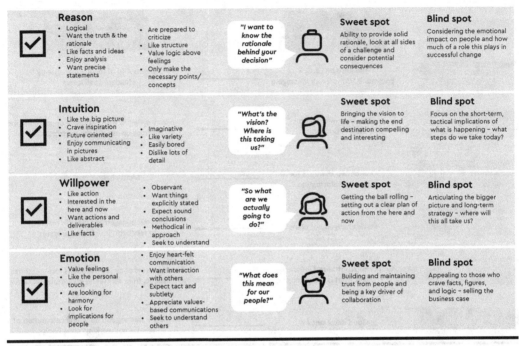

Figure 5.9 Different engagement and communication styles (Change Story Workshop).

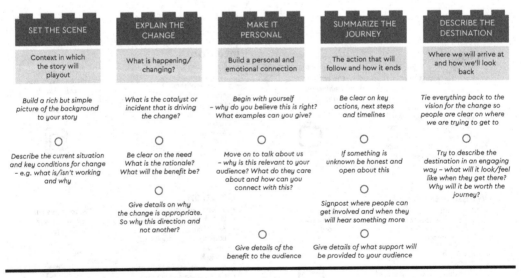

Figure 5.10 How to structure effective stories.

SET THE SCENE	EXPLAIN THE CHANGE	MAKE IT PERSONAL	SUMMARIZE THE JOURNEY	DESCRIBE THE DESTINATION
Context in which the story will play out	What is happening/changing?	Build a personal and emotional connection	The action that will follow and how it ends	Where we will arrive at and how we'll look back

If you were to share your story with your neighbor, would the reaction be: Interesting, tell me more? Or: Sorry, I stopped paying attention after the first few seconds?

Figure 5.11 How to structure effective stories (template).

Actions should come from the change impact analysis and your change story. The story can and should be used in communications materials, formal meeting, presentations, one-to-one conversations, etc.

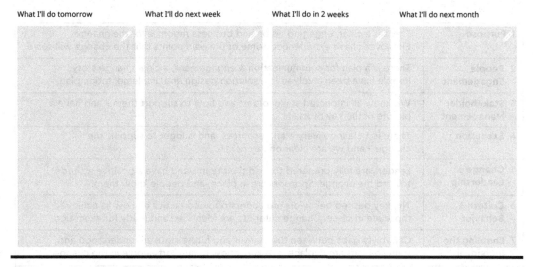

What I'll do tomorrow	What I'll do next week	What I'll do in 2 weeks	What I'll do next month

Figure 5.12 Committing to action.

Change Readiness Assessment

What Is It?

A change readiness assessment will provide you with insights into how ready your organization is for a change. By conducting a readiness assessment, you will identify how prepared the organization is for a particular change and which areas you can prepare even further. Change readiness is the ability to initiate and respond to change in ways that create advantage, minimize risk, and, at the same time, sustain performance. With this ambitious perspective, it's crucial to assess several dimensions of the impacted organization to get an understanding of how prepared it is for the upcoming change. We have distilled nine focus areas that all can be brought into play, or you can select from these the focus areas most important to your situation. The questions we ask within those areas will provide a picture of the level of change readiness and whether we have delivered enough activities within that space to ensure de-risking it. It will also clarify if there are there things we still need to do.

Here, we have questions we ask people to agree or disagree with or rate their level of readiness in each area. It is a way of deconstructing the overall level of activities to help us understand risk and what we have to do about it. The nine focus areas are shown in Figure 5.13 below.

Why It Matters?

A change readiness assessment is a critical component, as it will increase the chance of success with the change by providing guidance on what needs to be

1 Purpose	There is a clear, engaging vision and business rationale for the change. Employees have experienced some of the pain points that the change will solve.
2 People Engagement	There is a plan for communication & engagement, a clear change story. People have been involved in a solution design and implementation plan.
3 Stakeholder Management	We know all impacted stakeholders and how to support them – and have a picture of the key blockers.
4 Execution	There is a clear delivery plan, resources, and budget to support the change – and we are clear on key risks.
5 Change Leadership	Leaders are fully prepared to lead their teams and have a positive attitude toward the change. Sponsors are in place, and people know them.
6 Culture & Behavior	The key desired behaviors are understood and tactics on how to achieve those are in place. Change catalysts are identified and ready for execution.
7 Enabling the individual	Capability gaps between the current and future state are understood and training plans are in place. We know how to support people in the change.
8 Sustainability	A sustainability plan for how to track and communicate progress, benefits, and successes after the go-live.
9 Historical context	Previous changes have been implemented successfully and leaders have been active role models. Our employees are willing to embrace change.

Figure 5.13 9 Different focus areas of the Change Readiness Assessment.

done to prepare and ready impacted areas in the organization. Conducting a change readiness assessment will bring you to a more proactive position where you bring to light any misalignment or risks that need to be dealt with to ensure a successful change before you implement or release the change. From a timing perspective, it can be quite valuable to understand if the organization is ready to go live with, for example, ways of working or a new digital product.

How to Bring It into Action?

There are different approaches on how to bring this assessment into action by an organization. Is it to assess readiness to support change at a particular time in the future? Or is it to assess readiness right now, or maybe a combination of the two perspectives? So, it is important to be clear in the framing of the assessment whether it is readiness today or when we have delivered some activities further down the line. You can use it in both ways pragmatically if we have an indication today whether we are good to go or not. The other approach is to look, for example, one month ahead to what we think will be in place at that point in time and plan proactively what you need to do and achieve until that point in time.

One of the most efficient ways of assessing change readiness is to send out a change readiness survey. This allows you to gather information on any details unique to your organization that can help you assess how ready teams are for the change.

Alternatively, it can be used as a leadership dialogue tool where you discuss the different elements and utilize questions from the different categories. Depending on the session, who you are engaging, the level of detail, etc., you can either be very concrete and concise as you see it in the spreadsheet or you can be much more conversational as in a facilitated dialogue in a workshop.

There are two essential steps to consider when you are conducting a change readiness assessment:

1. Conduct the assessment – and adjust to the context and target groups as indicated above.
2. Be clear on the actions and initiatives that you will take based on the outcome of the assessment. When you ask people to assess focus areas like this, they will also expect specific actions to be taken to mitigate risks or cover areas that need to be further strengthened, in addition to feedback on their input.

In this example, you see the full dimension of the assessment covering the nine focus areas – and with correlating sub-questions for each focus area. Those questions can be rephrased and adjusted depending on who you are engaging with and the specific context, and which of the topics are most relevant depending on where you are in the change journey. This example could be targeted toward leaders and shared as prework prior to a leadership workshop, asking each leader to assess the level of change readiness based on their perspective and their business area. To validate the outcome, it would be meaningful to also hear the view of people in the teams, to see whether they have the same view. Below is an example of the assessment questions used in a leadership workshop (Figure 5.14).

Change Readiness Assessment: Questionnaire

		Strongly Disagree 1	2	3	4	Strongly Agree 5
	1# Purpose					
1	There is one clear, engaging vision for STM that all of our leaders can articulate			x		
2	The business rationale and case for the Change transformation is clear and compelling			x		
3	Employees have experienced the problems in their day-to-day work that XX (the change) is trying to solve					x
						3.7
	2# People Engagement					
4	There is a plan of how and when we will communicate with our people				x	
5	Our communications and engagement plan accounts for the varying needs of different audiences				x	
6	There is a process in place to get regular insight from our employees throughout the change			x		
7	We have a clear, logical and engaging story to tell about the change			x		
8	Employees have been involved in the solution design and implementation planning		x			
9	Employees 'buy-in' to the change and believe it is the right thing to do		x			
10	We have involved people at the earliest possible point in the change			x		
						3.0
	3# Stakeholder Management					
11	We know who all the impacted stakeholders are and we have plans to support them through the change				x	
12	We know who the key blockers or areas of resistance are and have plans to manage these				x	
						4.0
	4# Execution					
13	There is a clear delivery plan for the change				x	
14	There is enough resource & budget to support the delivery of the change			x		
15	We are clear on the key risks of the Change and we have a plan to mitigate them				x	
						3.7

Figure 5.14 Change Readiness Assessment: Questionnaire I.

5# Change Leadership

	1	2	3	4	5
16 Leaders feel fully prepared to lead their teams through the change				x	
17 Leaders have a positive attitude towards the Change and are supportive of what we are doing				x	
18 There is a sponsor for the Change and employees know who this is		x			
19 Our sponsor feels fully prepared to support the Change		x			
					3.0

6# Culture & Behaviour

	1	2	3	4	5
20 The key behaviour changes needed to support the Change are understood and plans are in place to achieve this				x	
21 The current culture and ways of working will be enablers for the Change				x	
22 We have identified change catalysts across our teams to help support the execution of the Change			x		
					3.7

7# Enabling the Individual

	1	2	3	4	5
23 Capability gaps between the current and future state are understood & training plans are in place to bridge these				x	
24 There are no other changes happening that will reduce the capacity of my business area to absorb the Change				x	
25 There are no 'after affects' of previous changes that could have a negative impact on the Change				x	
26 We know what support our employees need to get through the Change and we implement this in the delivery				x	
27 We are clear on the full impact of the Change on our employees and where this impact differs between people & teams			x		
28 Employees are clear on how the Change will affect their day-to-day work and what they can do to make it a success			x		
29 Employees know how their relationships (internally and externally) will change as a result of the Change					
					3.7

8# Sustainability

	1	2	3	4	5
30 We will be building & implementing a sustainability plan for after the the Change delivery		x			
31 We will be tracking and communicating benefits & success after the formal project closes		x			
32 We have already considered which 'business as usual' (BAU) practises need to change to support the Change	x				
					1.7

9# Historical Context

	1	2	3	4	5
33 Previous changes have been implemented successfully		x			
34 In previous changes, our leaders have been active role models and change leaders		x			
35 Our employees are willing to embrace change			x		
					2.3

Figure 5.14 Change Readiness Assessment: Questionnaire II (Continued)

In the following overview, you see examples of the outcome and results. And further below, leaders shared different levels of readiness in their teams. Here, it would be relevant to have dialogue on the different focus areas, sharing learnings and initiatives needed to succeed with the change. And, to ensure a dialogue and commitment to the actions and initiatives that are important to the outcome, you can focus the discussion:

- *"What is most important that you as individual leaders and as a leadership team are focused on based on the results of the Change Readiness Assessment?*
- *And what actions will you take?"*

In Figure 5.15 on page 71 you find another examples of how a condensed version of the focus areas was deployed for a digital initiative. The focus areas were translated into a more relevant context just before a business go-live with a new digital solution. Additionally, the questions were rephrased toward people in the teams being impacted by the change.

In this context, there was clear and very strong direction from the Steering Group that, together with assessment of the readiness of the new digital platform/system, they also wanted an assessment of the readiness of the team from a change perspective. Together, this should form and be the foundation for their go/no go decision for the go-live of the new digital solution. The approach here was to survey the team being impacted – followed up by a dialogue, as a natural part of the last training session, of how ready they feel and in which areas they were most comfortable and least comfortable.

The outcome of the change readiness assessments was a good understanding that the processes and ways of working needed to be even clearer. And naturally, doing the assessment was one thing, but it was another thing to identify the needed actions to be taken.

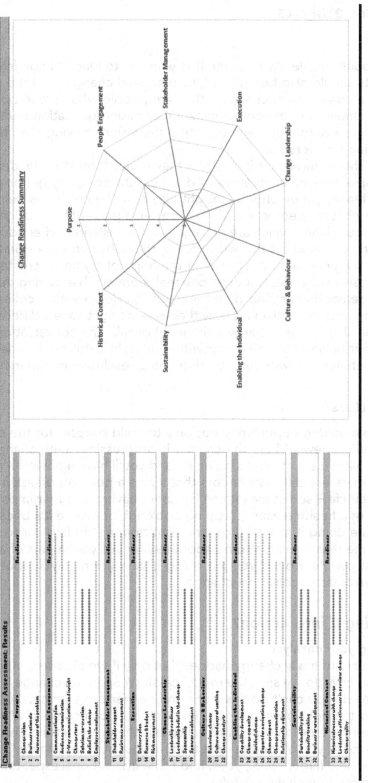

Figure 5.15   Change Readiness Summary.

Catch the Catalysts

What Is It?

Change is about people. As a leader, it is your job to lead change from the top. Your catalysts should also be on hand, helping lead change from the ground up. A catalyst is a champion of change – they are people who spread positive messages and counteract under-communication or misinterpretation during change. Catalysts play a key role in communicating the vision, making the change clear and compelling for everyone.

Catalysts should never act in secret – they're not "spies" for leaders. Instead, they are people who are uniquely placed to help the company get on board with change. For leaders, they offer an insight into how the change is being lived on the ground – what are people actually feeling, what parts of the change messages are getting through and which are getting lost in translation, where do they need more support, etc. And for the wider team, they offer an opportunity to share concerns with a peer in an open way in the hope of trying to create a solution that drives positive change. Not everyone feels comfortable sharing their feelings openly with senior leaders but might feel able to do so with a colleague. They can then either help to explain (as they themselves might have a different point of view they can share to help clarify a situation) or take the conversation further. It is an important balance to strike to identify the right catalysts and help them to achieve these functions, without it turning into an exclusive membership group.

Why It Matters?

Catalysts are a golden opportunity not only to build support for the change but to get a frontline view of how the change is progressing. With change champions, you will get a view of what's going on and you'll have a powerful channel for messaging. There are different factors that affect a person's decision to make a change in their life – sometimes it can be about having a bigger impact (e.g., on the climate), or a health reason (stopping smoking), or maybe it's because others around you are doing it as well (like switching from a standard car to an electric car). One of the reasons can also be about feeling like you're part of a collective movement. If people around you are doing it, and are highly supportive of the change, it can create a collective change.

How to Bring It into Action?

1. Identifying your catalyst

Catalysts can act to make change happen, but only if we choose the right people for the job. So how do we spot the model catalyst? Sparking change is more than a one-person job. You can't do this alone and neither can your catalysts. The first task is to find the right people for the job. Catalysts can come in all shapes and sizes. And there are no hard-and-fast rules, but there are certain characteristics that are sure to set you off on the right track in your hunt for change champions.

In this overview (Figure 5.16), you'll find some inspirational aspects to consider when looking for your change catalysts.

Figure 5.16 Identify your Change Catalysts.

Based on this overview, it's a productive exercise for leaders to take some time to consider who in their teams would be great change catalysts and what makes them a great choice.

2. Briefing your catalysts

Catalysts need to understand what their role entails. And it's your job as a leader to make sure your catalysts understand what it takes to drive change locally. It's useful for leaders to prepare and practice what the role will be. You will here find some inspirational points that can be used as additional tips on what the role of the catalyst is and how you can help by giving your change catalysts tactics for how to achieve their purpose.

- **Think outside of the box to make things real for the wider population.** As a catalyst you're trying to influence a bigger audience, so think about what they as a group might need help with in terms of messaging or belief. Do this by adopting a different perspective – imagine you're the other person and try to answer the question "Why am I seeing change in this way?"
- **Promote an infectious attitude toward change and start a movement.** Look out for positive change behavior and call it out when you see it. Help others feel recognized and feel like they are contributing.
- **Be curious, challenge negative opinions, and get to the root of the issues.** Sometimes you might be met with cynicism – take the time to have a conversation with these people to help identify where this resistance might be coming from, and help to steer them to a different direction by offering an alternative view. Remember to do this authentically, however!
- **Influence others to create a spark that will initiate change.** Sometimes, as a catalyst, you can spark a chain reaction by getting a small group on board, and then using them as mini-catalysts to drive the positive behaviors forward.
- **Test the water and see what's working and what isn't.** Don't be afraid to try a few different things out as you try to spread the message.
- **Be persistent** – change takes time to take hold, so don't give up,

It's important for catalysts to understand that their influence (peer influence) is powerful. Especially when it comes to building belief and helping teams feel listened to (Figure 5.17 on page 75).

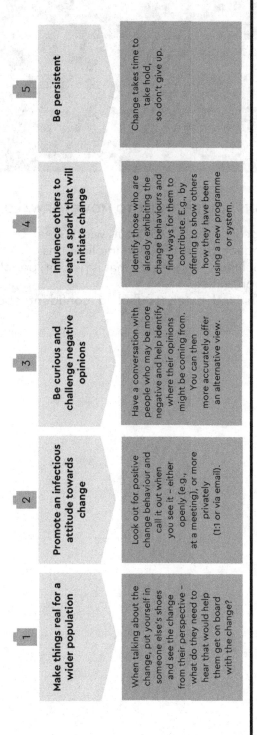

Figure 5.17 Briefing your Change Catalysts.

TOP TIPS – UNDERSTANDING THE CHANGE

1. Ensure the key stakeholders have a thorough understanding of the change and what it means for individuals.
2. Follow through with your promises. Don't let great insights go to waste – have a plan in place as to how you can make a difference.
3. Invest time in choosing the right people and letting them know why they're perfect for the job.

SIGNS YOU'RE READY TO MOVE FORWARD...

■ You have a change journey planned out, with a clear, broad understanding of the change impact, trade-offs, and implications.
■ You have a compelling change story that is helping people understand the reasons and opportunities.
■ You have leaders and catalysts feeling confident about dealing with change.

CASE STUDY: ELEMENT[2] DESIGN IN THE SPEED TO MARKET TRANSFORMATION

A strong and authentic change story was instrumental to create understanding of the need for change

**By Torsten Bjørn,
Senior Director in Element Design and System Governance**

CONTEXT OF THE ELEMENT DESIGN INITIATIVE

The Element Design initiative was a project stream within the Speed to Market Program.[3] The overall objective was to reduce the lead time in the Element Design process from Element Design and Development to Engineering.

In this case study, you will hear about Torsten Bjørn's journey to drive the change as a leader. The case study will focus on his approach to understand the change and how he was taking ownership of the change as a new leader of the team – as well as how he was leading the change. It will also spotlight how Bjørn created his narrative to explain the rationale and the benefits of the change, as an enabler to make people understand the change AND believe in it. Bjørn engaged with key stakeholders, employees, and other relevant people in the organization where his authentic change story played an influential role.

Bjørn is a very experienced, senior LEGO leader within Design and Development with strong and solid leadership experience and expertise built by heading up various areas within design and development. He has been a part of many of the transformations in the history of the LEGO Group and is very humble toward changes and transformation. He knows what it takes to make changes stick.

The Element Design and Speed to Market initiative was started by another People Leader heading up the Element Design Team. After some months, though, a leader rotation was made and Bjørn took over the leadership role for Element Design. Bjørn explains:

Getting Onboard

I took over the job as leader from a colleague, so I did not have many insights into this initiative. In the leadership team, I had heard and understood the overall objective of the Speed to Market initiative in Element Design. When I came onboard, an A3[4] was already established. I was quickly introduced to this initiative by the existing leaders, and I already sensed a need for further clarification on how to lead and create ownership of the change. One of the element development specialists in the team was having the role as the business owner and the existing leader explained to me that he, as a leader, was more in a sponsor role and was the connection to the Steering Committee.

I sensed very early in the process that there was a need to create more impact on the full leadership team in the area and on the organization as a whole. I considered how to get the full line of leaders involved to a greater extent. So this was one of the first initiatives that I focused on. A short time after this first introduction, it became very clear to me that this was not just a quick fix we could do in our team. This was much broader and more complex.

The overall change vision[5] was already in place – the case for change, "the why," and the overall objectives made a lot of sense to me, both in relation to improving ways-of-working and getting closer to the market. The difficult part was how to do this. To build integrated processes and to be able to accelerate by working smarter and not working harder was important, in a time with a huge workload in the organization and a rather low score on our People Pulse as to work–life balance. And as a principle, it is very ingrained in me to aim for working in a more intelligent way and still having high motivation and satisfaction from the people being impacted. So based on this direction, I was focused on reflecting and analyzing how the vision would impact my team and how to involve them in the best way.

I started by looking at the scope of the initiative and reached out to the different key stakeholders, like leaders from Engineering, to figure out how they saw the scope. The objective was to reduce the lead time significantly[6] for a specific part of the portfolio, so we needed to be clear and aligned as this was impacting end-to-end processes across teams. I could see benefits in working on the full portfolio to simplify the approach – and to have a holistic view of the complexity and to create maximum impact. This resulted in an extra leadership loop on the scoping to create understanding and motivation to make an implementation on the full portfolio. In parallel with creating a common picture of the scope, there was the task of getting the right people involved in this as well. Kaizen workshops were planned, but it was crucial to get the right people involved to represent the end-to-end understanding and to have the needed knowledge present in the workshops and, not the least, to involve and empower key players to create the future ways of working together. As leaders, we joined the workshops to understand the pain points and ways-of-working – and to be there in situations of scope clarification. That was greatly needed. A couple of times during the first Kaizen workshop we actually needed to "take a time-out" to have some high-level and tough discussions to provide the right aligned direction for the team,

I could see the need and the value in investing time to understand how we were working today – and, comparing this to the vision and the overall direction, I was curious whether there were any blind spots to be aware of. One thing was the descriptions in the A3; during the first workshops it became clear that there were more and bigger pain points than indicated from the start. So, to be able to reduce the lead time, it was important for me to understand the root causes of the pain points. I was convinced that if we could resolve the pain points then reducing the lead time would follow.

Go-Look-See Approach with a Curious Mindset

A way to understand the current behaviors and ways of working was to join and participate in the Kaizen workshops together with a team of specialists within different parts of the processes. As a supplement to this, Bjørn joined many different daily operational sessions, planning and prioritization meetings, assessment sessions, etc., in different team sessions. This was done to make some deep dives into the pain points he identified to really understand the change and its impact.

> I recall that one of the first issues that was explained to me when I was getting introduced to all this was that in "Simplify to Grow,"[7] everyone relied on a former Technical Lead role. And now it all had landed on our table to take the Technical Lead role, managing and driving the process. And that explanation came up many times in different contexts and fora. And to be honest, I became a little bit tired of listening to this excuse. There must have been a good explanation and reason for changing this setup. And instead of pointing fingers, I used one of our LEGO Leadership Behaviors around curiosity. So I was curious and demonstrated that curiosity to understand why the change had been made and what benefits were implied in this solution. And I was coming in as a new leader, so it was easy for me to be curious in a natural way.
>
> Based on the many go-look-sees, workshops, one-to-one dialogues with key players in the process, etc., I gathered the needed data and insights into the current ways of working. And I was very surprised about the many different stakeholders involved – different levels of stakeholders and complexities created in the process which is one of our core development processes. We have developed elements over many years and I have previously been close to the process – and I was really surprised about the level of complexity that had been created. No doubt that the intensive growth of the company over many years had resulting in many subprocesses and new people and teams coming on board. And I could see that the go-look-sees were really a good investment to be prepared for the more formalized workshops. So there were a couple of months where I really got insights into the pain points and how to move forward.

Being Ahead of the Change as a Leader

> When you see the need for a change and initiate a change, I am very aware that as a leader you need to be 80% or more ahead of your people and your team to understand why we are doing this. I have learned from previous experiences that as a leader you need to invest up-front in understanding the change. If you do not understand the change, overseeing some critical elements of the

change, it becomes more challenging to set the scene for why we are doing this and being able to explain the change, and getting people and the organization to follow you.

I remember one of my first meetings with the leadership team where the project lead and business owner were presenting an update on the project. I clearly sensed that there was no buy-in from the others in my leadership team – there was no enthusiasm in the team in relation to the initiative. I explained that the change would impact all our processes and the collaboration with all stakeholders, and to succeed with the change we needed to act as one team on this.

At this point of time, I really sensed that we did not have sufficient power in this, so the business owner, project lead, and I had a dialogue and I explained that it is great that they were managing this transformation, but we needed to have the rest of the leadership team with us. They needed to be a part of this, taking ownership and supporting implementation of the changes. We discussed different ways of engaging the leadership team and "the art of delegation and empowerment" – and how to ensure that we considered this as a task that we were accountable for together.

Getting the Right People on Board

It was not only at the leader level that Bjørn needed to get more people on board, but also more specialists were needed to ensure that this was not just becoming a theoretical leader case but a practical approach with specialists having the needed knowledge and skills on daily operations and ways of working. Additionally, to lead the change from the bottom-up, Bjørn needed to have the right change catalysts onboard.

In changes I am leading, I look into diversity and whether there are people on the team representing something that I do not represent myself. And you should dare to challenge the status quo. During the initial period of time when I came on board, I made some adjustments as to who to support and help lead the change in the organization. It is important that you dare to challenge what you do today and, if you want to create benefits and value, then you should be prepared for a level of unpopularity. This can be a challenge, as it is easiest to just continue to do what we do today. And that is where you need to be able to think holistically and have the overview and the knowledge, so you are not stuck in the existing ways of doing things. You need to dare to change and to dare to think outside of the box.

There were a couple of people struggling with their thinking and, at that point of time, we got a newly hired engineer onto the team who could really think out of the box, and he was not locked in the current ways of working. That brought a lot of value to the process. And it was valuable to have a good mix of different profiles as change catalysts on the team based on different seniorities, those knowing the business and the tasks well, and those who were strong in communicating the change and explaining the why as well as the benefits of the change.

In the team, we succeeded in breaking down the change into smaller elements and delegated those to the different change agents and leaders on the leadership team when we were ready to implement. The leaders were acting as both functional and cross-functional implementation leads and that actually resulted in shifting to a totally different gear having the full leadership team on board with each of their accountabilities. So the team of change agents took a very important role together with the leadership team to make the change become a reality.

The Change Story as a Key Enabler

It was a very complex stakeholder landscape. Bjørn and the team needed to get involved and lead the change together with the most creative team in the development process from engineering to operations. It required a lot of effort to get the different and diverse key stakeholders on board and to understand and support the change. Bjørn explains how he used his very authentic change story as a powerful way to create awareness and buy-in to the change in the organization.

I was highly inspired by having a better structure on the change journey with the different change and engagement activities, and I started up by building awareness through a narrative that in a very short and concise way could explain the why, what, and how. I also became aware of how important it was to make it personal. It is so easy to go into too many details and elaborate too much on certain specifics, but having those five key points[8] to stick to and to repeat again and again helped me get the storyline straight which created consistency in how the storyline was delivered in different contexts.

Finding the key element in the storyline that would make it personal was important, but what could it be? I have been working in the LEGO Group for many years, so the fact that I, as a veteran leader, could be so surprised when diving into the process realizing how complex the processes had become – and how complex we have set up structures and ways of working. This was the part that became my personal and emotional element in the storyline. Early in the process I could feel that this gave me something that felt right. When we started getting data, I was very surprised that the process was not anchored and executed in one place, but in different areas with six to seven different subprocesses. Also, from a leadership perspective, it became personal for me. This was our own leadership

allowing for all these subprocesses instead of thinking more holistically and end-to-end, which was an important point for me.

So the personal part started surfacing and became clear along
with the data that was generated. By understanding the complexity of our ways of working, based on the analysis work, we could
move forward to work on the current pain points. My own internal-
ization and understanding of the processes was the foundation of
the personal way of explaining the change. So it came up in a very
natural way. And so did the resolution of the pain points. We should
not use 53 spreadsheets to plan an element – we should be able to
set this up in one common system. We are not interested in creating spreadsheets, but our objective is to develop LEGO elements in
a good and intelligent way, and also look for value and motivation
instead of just creating another spreadsheet.

Additionally, I also used the LEGO values[9] to act as one team and
use our common muscle to succeed in this.

Engagement at All Levels in the Organization

Bjørn invested a lot of time and engaged stakeholders at different levels in
the organization to make sure that a similar understanding of the situation
and the pain points was understood by the key stakeholders.

I was quite inspired by the structured way we did our stakeholder
mapping and I realized early in the process that if we did not succeed in getting the stakeholders with us in this, it would be difficult. So I started from the top and worked my way down in the
organization. Especially in the beginning, I had many both formal
and informal coffee check-ins to create awareness of the initiative
and what we had on the agenda. And, particularly, with the Project
Management network and the leaders, leading all the novelty projects had a high level of attention from my side as they were instrumental in making this happen.

In my leadership team, I introduced the approach to make their
own change stories together with the change playbook, and that
gave the team even more awareness of the storyline and which
anchor points we had. This is often the part that you skip as it is
difficult and takes time. But it was very powerful that we were clear
on the same elements in the storyline. In the different engagement
sessions, the storyline was recognizable and it was clear that we
worked together in the same framework. That created a strong
confidence and belief in the change.

Together with my leadership team, we ensured that this transformation was on the agenda in all our monthly calls with the full
organization. We gave updates on the latest progress and when
more people were involved we gave more detailed introductions

and got them involved to a bigger and bigger extent. Additionally, we arranged workshops for the extended leadership where we were looking into mutual dependencies, so we ensured that we were not chasing the same issues and we connected the dots together.

Final Leader Reflections

This transformation was a great experience and achievement – one of the best I have been leading. We ended up not only reducing the lead time significantly for part of the portfolio but for the full portfolio. My experience of zooming in first (based on, for example, the go-look-sees in the beginning) and then zooming out again to involve and empower my team was powerful. It gave me something personal when looking at the task and created the case for change based on factual data instead of being subjective. I am sure that the team and my colleagues could sense that I was passionate about this. I see that it is super important to consider as a leader when you should go into the details and when to delegate and empower. By going into the details yourself, it easily becomes your own project and this was also based on some of my earlier experiences. But this time, I decided that the approach should be different. So by engaging and empowering my team and the organization and key stakeholders – and ensuring that they also had "shining eyes" in this – this is how we succeeded. It was tough and we learned a lot, that we as leaders can use in the future.

Notes

1. Vision Statement described in Chapter 4.
2. A universal name for a LEGO Brick. Also, in technical terms, often considered to refer to a piece of a specific shape and color (e.g., a black 1×1 plate is a different element than a blue 1×1 plate).
3. You can read more about the context of the Speed to Market Program in Chapter 2.
4. A3 is a problem solving tool describing the problem, root causes, countermeasures, etc.
5. The Change Vision for Speed to Market you can find in Chapter 4.
6. No further quantified data is given here as this is considered sensitive data.
7. *Simplify to Grow* is one of the bigger LEGO transformations; see more in Chapter 2.
8. Referring to the Change Story Template on page 64.
9. Referring to the LEGO People Promise: "Together we succeed" – you can read more in Chapter 1.

CHAPTER 6

MOMENT 3 – PERSONALIZING THE CHANGE

What Is It?

The point where all affected people make sense of the change and how it relates to their own motivations and aspirations. The aim is to get each person to feel not just aware, but positive, directly involved, and responsible – and thinking about how they need to be different. This may be an elastic moment that needs revisiting over time.

Possible signs that indicate we need to get ready to change

- People talk about what "they" are doing when speaking about the changes – rather than what "I" am doing
- Some people show little curiosity about the change
- The people who are eager start feeling like the exception

How people are feeling

- "I'm really enthusiastic"
- "I'll get started right away"
- "I'm curious – I think this new world could be good for me"
- "I'm passive – I'll just do what I'm told to do"
- "I'm disinterested – it's not something that will really affect me"
- "I'm ignoring it and hopefully it will go away"
- "I'm scared – I can only see the downside for me"

DOI: 10.4324/9781003243113-6

Why It Matters?

If we get this moment right, we'll get:

- Intrinsic motivation to change
- A critical mass of people ready to change
- A positive buzz
- Confident uncertainty

If we don't get it right:

- Paralyzing uncertainty/fear
- Disconnection with change
- Confusion and people making up their own rules
- Saboteurs

WHERE AND HOW CAN YOU HAVE THE BIGGEST IMPACT?

To succeed with this moment, you must support leaders who provide honesty and clarity about the facts – the non-negotiables and what individuals can control. You must find the time to make the change relevant to the individual and their own situation and help them place themselves within their reality. This can help to create a sense of ownership and autonomy which in turn drives positive change behavior. Make it clear where you expect them to contribute so they are empowered and don't feel the change is done *to* them but *with* them. Make sure you are ready and prepared to manage different emotional reactions to change and even ready to have difficult dialogues in an honest and authentic way and with a sense of empathy for how these messages impact others.

Where	How
Facilitate sense-making as a group and provide a means for each person to internalize the change and create a personal change map to see themselves in the change. Providing insights and understanding of how individuals can build up personal resilience to navigate yourself and lead others in the change.	Make-It-Mine Workshop page 86 Change Campfires page 107 Personal Resilience page 109
Change is hard as we as human beings are "hard-wired" to favor control, and we are all different and complex, and therefore our reactions are different and unpredictable. Understand why change is hard, different emotional reactions, and how to manage those reactions.	Managing Emotional Reactions page 123
Prepare yourself to face difficult conversations with courage and confidence and not shy away from reality. Discover how to master your emotions and stay in control.	Courageous Conversations page 130

Make It Mine

What Is It?

It's important that we take the time to make the change feel relevant to us and to the individuals on our team and help them understand their role in the change. By doing this, we can help them create a sense of ownership and independence, which in turn drives positive change behavior.

Why It Matters?

If we get this moment right, we'll get:
Tactics for how you and your team can help personalize the change, including:

- Getting individuals on the team to personalize the change by thinking about what their motives are, where they can take some control over the change (not feeling it is being "done *to* them"), and what might incentivize them to get on-board.
- Identifying how your world will change and what this means for your key stakeholder relationships.
- Exploring what your individual change journey looks like.
- Understanding your style of motivation, and how you can use this to help influence others and drive forward.

If we don't get it right:
- Unlike earlier tools where the focus was on working out the big picture vision and story, these tools are focused on helping people apply this to their day-to-day reality. Not fully understanding the change or not internalizing it can lead to confusion and people making up their own rules rather than working together toward a common goal. There may be impacted teams that you have not engaged with or have not included in the journey, resulting in feelings of exclusion and people not feeling as though they are part of the change.

How to Bring It into Action?

The Make-It-Mine sessions can each be run in their entirety within 3–4 hours, or 1–2 hours depending on the size of the team or length of dialogue/sharing elements. There are four different bite-size options for team engagement sessions:

In case of time restrictions, each session can be run as a stand-alone exercise. When running exercises stand-alone, you take some time at the start to still do an introduction and/or a recap of what was done beforehand to link the sessions together in the minds of the participants. To pick the right sessions for you and your team, review the key points in each session, which gives you a high-level overview of the aim for that part of the session.

In the following, you will find inspirational facilitation guides for each of the sessions. You can take out sub-sections and combine, but also bear in mind that you must create a good flow for participants, allowing people to internalize, discuss, and have time for meaningful dialogues and reflections. In both the first session, "Make-It-Mine," and the second session, "Build your change journey," you will find

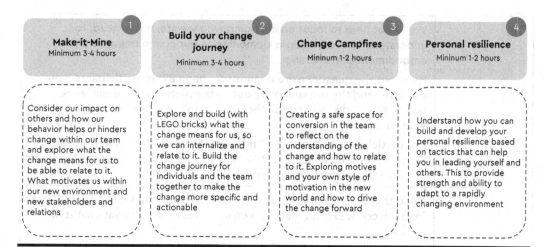

Figure 6.1   Make It Mine – 4 different bite-size team activities.

cases and stories with real-life examples and learning to provide practice lenses on how these sessions were brought into play (see Figure 6.1).

Activity 1: Make-It-Mine Workshop
Inspirational Facilitation Overview

Introduction Make It Mine – the importance of personalizing the change	Key point: To introduce the topic and ensure participants understand why they're here today.
	Start by explaining the topic of the session and the specific outcome.
	Explain that one of the reasons why change can be difficult is that it can feel like it is being done *to us*, not *with us*. Often decisions are made at senior levels and by the time they have been filtered down to us and our teams, it can feel like we have no control over the change, or any say in the matter at all.
	For many large, strategic changes, we won't have much control over the decisions that are being made. But what we do have control over is how we use the changing environment around us to our advantage, what opportunities we find within it, and how we make sense of the change for us and our situation.
Our impact on others	Key point: To consider our impact on others and how our behavior helps or hinders change within our team.
	Points to explain:
	• The way people perceive us is based on how we behave
	• Our behavior translates to our team, so it's important to think about how our actions embody change and how we can role-model and champion it as leaders
	• Awareness of our behaviors and actions can help us get more out of our relationships – this is especially important when we're going through change as our networks may shift and there's a need to build new relationships as a result

<table>
<tr>
<td></td>
<td>We're not here to focus on changing who we are, but instead, to understand how our actions demonstrate our commitment to and embodiment of the change.

Hand out the questionnaire (Figure 6.2 , page 89) to participants (you can also send the questionnaire out to the participants as pre-work before the workshop and ask them to complete it prior to the workshop).

Ask participants to spend 5–10 minutes completing the questionnaire. They should allocate a total of 10 points for each question, splitting them as they like across the three answers.</td>
</tr>
<tr>
<td></td>
<td>Once they have completed the questions, they should calculate the total for each color. Explain that each color represents a motivational style:

Red: Carer

Yellow: Driver

Blue: Professional

Green: Adapter (the Adapter is a combination of the other three)

Calculating results:

- If they have a score of 45 or more in a single color column, that column is their motivational style.
- If they have one score above 32 and one below 23, the style is a blend.
- If they have a score between 23 and 44 for each, the style is an adapter.</td>
</tr>
<tr>
<td></td>
<td>**Show Figure 6.3, page 90: "My motivational style – different styles"** and go through each of the motivational styles in turn, using the information in the slides and the handout, which includes:

- *Best bits*: key strengths for this style
- *Too much of a good thing*: where this style can create tension or blocks during this change
- *What they bring to a team*: strengths of this style within teams and where to apply these (e.g., "the perfect person if…")</td>
</tr>
</table>

For each question, allocate a total of 10 points across the 3 statements depending on your preferences.

01. I really like it when...
- ☐ Things are done correctly
- ☐ Things are done in a friendly/ supportive manner
- ☐ I've achieved something different

02. I really dislike it when I feel that I'm doing something...
- ☐ Unprofessional
- ☐ Unsociable
- ☐ Boring

03. It would really bother me if I lost...
- ☐ My independence
- ☐ My allies or friends
- ☐ My get up and go

04. I love having time to...
- ☐ Do something properly
- ☐ Get to know new people
- ☐ Take on new challenges

05. I like...
- ☐ Getting on with things
- ☐ Being in the middle of things
- ☐ Being in charge

06. I mostly appreciate praise when it...
- ☐ Comes from an expert
- ☐ Comes from the heart
- ☐ Comes from results

07. I am at my best when...
- ☐ I'm working out the solution to a difficult question
- ☐ I'm helping others
- ☐ I'm making things happen

08. I value...
- ☐ Freedom
- ☐ Friendship
- ☐ Results

09. The best decisions are made...
- ☐ Based on facts
- ☐ Collaboratively
- ☐ Decisively

10. My motto is...
- ☐ If a job's worth doing, it's worth doing properly
- ☐ Treat others as you would like to be treated
- ☐ Actions speak louder than words

TOTALS ☐ ☐ ☐

Figure 6.2 My Motivational Style (questionnaire).

Carer	Driver	Professional	Adapter
Best Bits	**Best Bits**	**Best Bits**	**Best Bits**
Honest, sincere, supportive, friendly, sociable.	Direct, competitive, excitable, fast, decisive, challenging.	Independent, rigorous, self-contained, thorough, accurate.	Flexible, collaborative, mediator, adaptable, jack-of-all-trades.
Too much of a good thing	**Too much of a good thing**	**Too much of a good thing**	**Too much of a good thing**
Simple-minded, naive, smothering, demanding, snooping.	Harsh, aggressive, superficial, inflexible, argumentative.	Aloof, nit-picky, cold, long-winded, fussy.	Weak, political, all-pleasing, convictionless, master of none.
What they bring to a team	**What they bring to a team**	**What they bring to a team**	**What they bring to a team**
• A Carer's foremost desire is for harmony with whatever group of people they are in, be it their family, their team at work or a group of friends	• Drivers are motivated by challenge, excitement and getting things done. They want to get to the point fast and, ideally, first. And then on to the next thing, and then the next	• Professionals are motivated by doing something very well–they want the best possible solution and, once they commit, they will be inclined to do whatever it takes to get it	• Adapters are people who are a combining of the other three styles. They see the merits in focusing on people, on getting things done and on quality
• They enjoy working with people	• They like to have demanding goals with clear outcomes and, preferably, a competitive element	• The professional's mantra is the saying: "If the job's worth doing, it's worth doing properly"	• They value flexibility and take a balanced approach to any situation
• They are naturally social, friendly and they make a real effort to get to know someone			
• They are also often very effective networkers			
The perfect person if... you want something done sensitively.	**The perfect person if...** you want something done quickly.	**The perfect person if...** you want something done 'properly'.	**The perfect person if...** you want to manage all possible eventualities.

Figure 6.3 My Motivational Style – different styles.

	Group discussion: • How do you think the four different action styles can be of benefit during the planned change? • Where could they present challenges? **Self-reflection:** • Share the "My motivational style" handout (Figure 6.4). Either individually or in pairs, ask participants to take some time and consider their motivational style and how it might impact how they react to or work within change. Using "if...then" planning, they should consider what they see as their biggest risk/opportunity for their style and what actions they could take around this. This could either be around how to prevent themselves from slipping into blocking behavior or how to capitalize on their style to drive positive change behavior in others. **Figure 6.4, page 91, My Motivational style – my tactics**
	Some examples may be as follows: **Carer:** "*If*... my tendency towards wanting to create harmony is actually preventing us from making a key decision within the change... *then* I'll be more direct about my intentions and conscious about steering the conversation. **Driver:** "*If*... I notice that my team isn't able to keep up with the pace I'm setting... *then* I'll revisit the goals and timelines I've set for achieving change and talk to them about where they need more support and care.

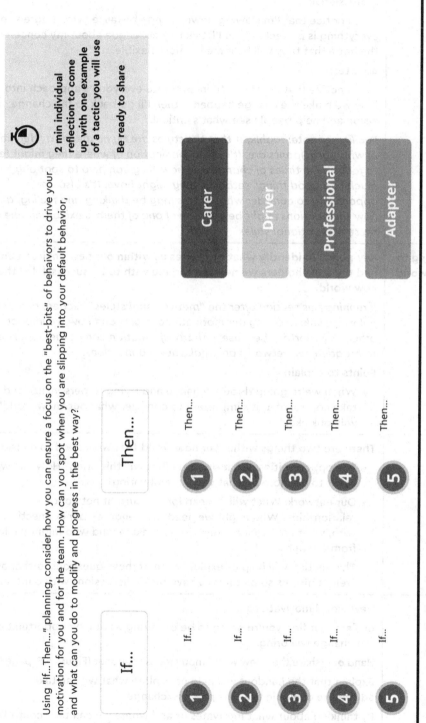

Using "If...Then..." planning, consider how you can ensure a focus on the "best-bits" of behaviors to drive your motivation for you and for the team. How can you spot when you are slipping into your default behavior, and what can you do to modify and progress in the best way?

2 min individual reflection to come up with one example of a tactic you will use

Be ready to share

If...

Then...

Carer

Driver

Professional

Adapter

Figure 6.4   My Motivational Style – my tactics.

	Professional: "*If*... I notice that I'm slowing down change because I won't agree until everything is perfect... *then* I'll talk to a colleague about my concerns in the hope that they will help me be more flexible. **Adapter:** "*If*... I notice that I'm trying to incorporate everyone's approach into how we make the change happen... *then* I'll go back to the change vision and help people see what's critical. *Facilitator note: Highlight that the styles are by no means a "definition" of who participants are. It's just an indication of where they might tend to focus on in times of change and how they can help to spot any "too much of a good thing" setbacks they might have. It's also an opportunity to consider what others may be thinking and feeling, and how their actions might be because of one of them is exhibiting one of these motivational styles.*
Connecting to our new world	**Key point: To identify what motivates us within our new environment and the stakeholders we need to engage with to be successful in the new world.** *If running this section after the "motivational styles" section, make the following link: Knowing our motivational styles and how we impact others is important because with transformation comes the opportunity to broaden our networks and make new connections.* **Points to explain** • When we're going through change and trying to personalize and take control of it, it's important to consider what our "new world" will look like.
	There are two things within our new world that we'll need to consider: • The opportunities: What opportunities will this bring? How can we use it to do more of what we find motivating? • Our network: What will it mean for our current network/relationships? Who might we need to strengthen our connection with, what new connections are we making, and who might we lose from our network? • This section will help us explore both of these questions further as well as give us some tools to have these discussions with our teams.
	New world motivations **Explain** that first you're going to be exploring what new opportunities the change will bring. **Hand out/share** the "New world motivations" handout (Figure 6.5, page 93). **Explain** that the handout will help us explore what we can take advantage of within the new process/change. By thinking about what motivates us and where we can take control of the change, we can help personalize the change for us.

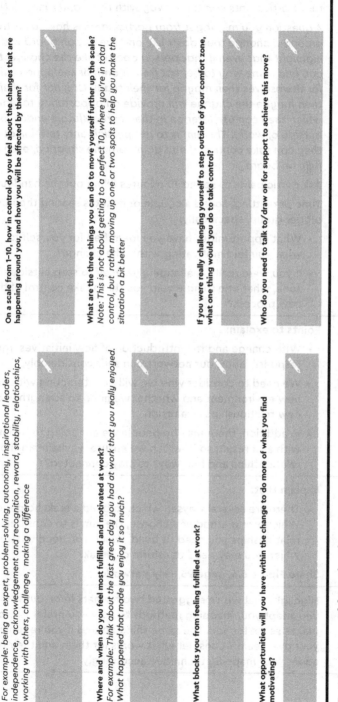

What motivates you?
For example: being an expert, problem-solving, autonomy, inspirational leaders, independence, acknowledgement and recognition, reward, stability, relationships, working with others, challenge, making a difference

Where and when do you feel most fulfilled and motivated at work?
For example: Think about the last great day you had at work that you really enjoyed. What happened that made you enjoy it so much?

What blocks you from feeling fulfilled at work?

What opportunities will you have within the change to do more of what you find motivating?

On a scale from 1–10, how in control do you feel about the changes that are happening around you, and how you will be affected by them?

What are the three things you can do to move yourself further up the scale?
Note: This is not about getting to a perfect 10, where you're in total control, but rather moving up one or two spots to help you make the situation a bit better

If you were really challenging yourself to step outside of your comfort zone, what one thing would you do to take control?

Who do you need to talk to/draw on for support to achieve this move?

Figure 6.5 My new world motivations.

	Facilitator notes: Make sure to highlight that this is also a great exercise that participants can take away with them and run with their teams. *A question you might get from participants is how to motivate someone around a change they don't like and are not on board with. In this case, highlight that even if that person doesn't like the change, they usually can find some way to benefit from it and/or see opportunity in it, if not for themselves then maybe for their team. Or if not for their current role, then maybe the change will provide an opportunity to learn new skills which they can use later on in their career/future endeavors (or even outside of work). The aim is to get participants to think about what they can take control of and gain from the situation, even if they're not fully on board.* **Ask** participants to spend 10 minutes filling out the handout. Time permitting, spend a couple of minutes sharing thoughts with the bigger group, specifically: • What opportunities have you identified for yourself to do more of what you find motivating within the change? • If you were really challenging yourself to step outside of your comfort zone, what one thing would you do to take control of the change/new process?
New Relations and stakeholder mapping	**Points to explain:** • With change and the introduction of new initiatives, roles, and responsibilities, our network can shift considerably. • We need to consider who we will be interacting with most in our new environment and whether we need to strengthen or create any new relationships as a result. • In addition, there may be people we are going to be interacting less with as a result, so how can we ensure we maintain those relationships and find ways to stay connected?
	Explain that: • There are several ways in which to build a stakeholder map. Whichever method you choose, the aim is to consider which relationships you need to build, which you need to strengthen, and which you may need to reform or break. **Share Figure 6.6, page 95 – My network.**
	Highlight that we've suggested two formats here, but it's important that you adapt your mapping methods to how you prefer to work and what makes sense for you. The same thing applies if you're running this with your own team – consider what works for them and their reality and adapt your mapping technique accordingly.

With the introduction of new initiatives, roles and responsibilities, it's important that those affected by change take the time to consider what their new world will look like. There are several ways in which to build a stakeholder map. The aim is to consider which relationships you need to build, which you need to strengthen, and which you may need to reform or break. You also need to consider which relationships remain unchanged.

To do this, use one of the two options below, and flex them to suit you and/or your team.

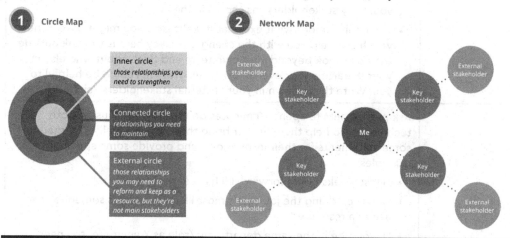

Figure 6.6   My network.

	Circle mapping:
	• For this technique, we consider our "circles of influence" – in our "inner circle" are those relationships we need to strengthen. This may be either new relationships you need to form, or maybe you find out you're working more closely with a new department/team, so you need to strengthen that existing relationship.
	• In your "connected circle" you have those relationships you need to maintain – so while circumstances may not have changed for you and that stakeholder, it's still important you focus your attention on them so you don't lose them with the shift in your network.
	• In your "external circle" are those relationships you may need to reform and keep as a resource, but they're no longer main stakeholders. Sometimes, these can be close relationships you used to have which, due to shifting work patterns, you're now not going to be working as much with. Consider how to ensure you don't lose the connection entirely as they can still offer valuable advice down the line. Maybe you can use them as an external mentor or a go-to for bigger strategic questions.

	Network mapping: • For this technique, instead of identifying whether you need to strengthen or maintain relationships at the start, you first spend time just identifying who your key stakeholders are going to be. • Start by drawing a circle that says, "Me". Then, build this out with your "key stakeholders" as shown in the image. • Then, think about what external stakeholders you might have or need which can help you with the change. The key here is to think outside the box – look beyond your own team and think about who else in your department or even in other departments could be helpful to you. Write these down in your "external stakeholders" circles.
	Ask participants to spend 10 minutes doing a test map, using both techniques. To help them further bring their network to life, by sharing some statements for their inspiration – and provide some specific examples: • "Most weeks going forward, I'll have a meeting with…" • "X will be doing the job that's most like mine, and is someone I can use as a resource." • "I won't be in the same department/role as X anymore, so I need to ensure I keep them in my extended network as they have key experience I need." • "Although I won't work with X going forward, I value their advice and input." • "If I need specific help, my new support person will be X" (i.e., process support, strategic input, technical liaisons).
Exploring my change map	This a very tactical and specific summary where participants can explore, reflect, and record with input from previous dialogues and reflections – and that can be used as a handout for participants. If it is a bigger team, you can break out into smaller teams and reflect together, or it can also be used as an individual exercise. It can also be used as post-work after the session is completed and be included in 1:1 dialogues between individuals and leaders or in a campfire session. This is a central element in personalizing the change – and is a great dialogue tool that encourages individuals to relate to the change and take accountability for their own change journey.
	Explain and brief participants on the different elements of "My Change Journey." Show Figure 6.7, page 97 – or use it as hand-out. • How do I feel about the change? • What does this mean for me? • What relationships does this impact? • What motivates me? Find the format and approach that you find most appropriate for the team to work with their reflections.
Wrap-up	General follow-up and closing

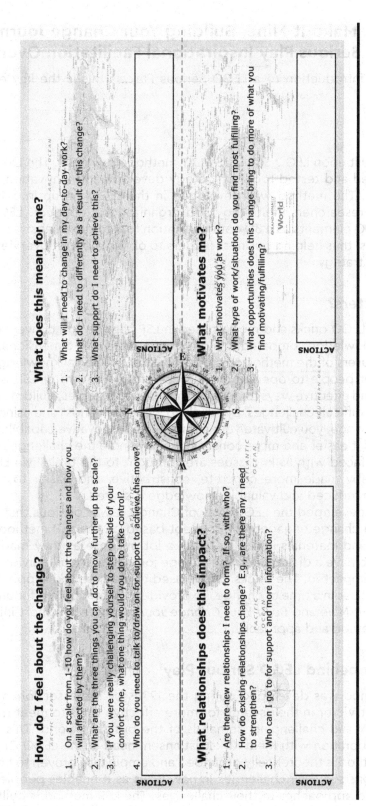

How do I feel about the change?

1. On a scale from 1–10 how do you feel about the changes and how you will affected by them?
2. What are the three things you can do to move further up the scale?
3. If you were really challenging yourself to step outside of your comfort zone, what one thing would you do to take control?
4. Who do you need to talk to/draw on for support to achieve this move?

ACTIONS

What relationships does this impact?

1. Are there new relationships I need to form? If so, with who?
2. How do existing relationships change? E.g., are there any I need to strengthen?
3. Who can I go to for support and more information?

ACTIONS

What does this mean for me?

1. What will I need to change in my day-to-day work?
2. What do I need to do differently as a result of this change?
3. What support do I need to achieve this?

ACTIONS

What motivates me?

1. What motivates you at work?
2. What type of work/situations do you find most fulfilling?
3. What opportunities does this change bring to do more of what you find motivating/fulfilling?

ACTIONS

Figure 6.7 My change map.

Activity 2: Make-It-Mine, Building Your Change Journey, and LEGO Serious Play Inspirational Facilitation Overview

Here first an introduction to a LEGO Serious Play as this is the key element of Activity 2.

What Is It?

This part is built upon LEGO SERIOUS PLAY methodology (LSP). The LSP approach is a recognized and tested tool for strategy development, innovation, and team development. The method was developed in the LEGO Group in collaboration with leading researchers in strategy and organizational conduct. LEGO Serious Play uses LEGO elements as a 3D communication tool to tackle abstract and complex problems, thus helping business leaders to obtain a better overview of organization and strategy.

Why It Matters?

The dynamic LEGO bricks and models used in LSP capture and convey remarkable amounts of knowledge compared to more standardized one-dimensional methods. This enables users of the method to create constructive social knowledge systems that empower people to operate more successfully. The aim of LSP is to create imaginative and effective ways to develop innovative strategies, build strong teams, and deal with difficult challenges. By "thinking with your hands" and using the LEGO brick as a language, you cultivate your creativity and innovative capabilities.

LSP makes it easier and more constructive to handle the challenges that organizations are faced with as key issues are "brought to the table" via LEGO models and thereby made more concrete, constructive, and easier to work with. Complexity is reduced and valuable knowledge is shared.

When we developed the LEGO Way of Change, it was obvious that we would be creating a change engagement concept based on the LSP method. Bringing LEGO bricks and materials into play made a lot of sense as they made it easier and simpler to have a dialogue on the change journey both for individuals and for teams being impacted. The bricks can be used to mediate and support the more difficult dialogues in a time of change. To provide a better context for understanding the *Make-It-Mine* and *Build Your Change Journey*, here is a short introduction to the LSP method and approach.

The Theory behind LEGO Serious Play[1]

The LSP method was developed during the 1990s by Professor Johan Roos and Professor Bart Victor in their search for more effective ways to meet the increasingly complex and challenging demands of the business world. This was done in close collaboration with Kjeld Kirk Kristiansen, head of the LEGO Group at the time. The method is theoretically grounded and empirically proven to help people in organizations see their challenges in new ways as it enables people to create new ideas and approaches to their challenges. The LSP method is built around a relatively simple number of elements and rules. If the method is facilitated in a skillful way, it can be useful to anyone who wants to engage in a more accessible, innovative, creative, and effective development process.

What Is Serious Play?

You might consider the term "serious play" to be a bit self-contradictory as play is often considered a frivolous leisure activity that is not suited for real and serious work. However, play is far from only a frivolous activity. Research shows that "play" has several business-related benefits. We relax our need for control – becoming more open-minded. This gives room for imagination so we can better imagine new solutions and see ourselves in new situations. Additionally, it improves our capacity to develop relationships. The literature on play concludes that play always serves a purpose, and for that reason, the purpose, the objectives, and/or the goals of the organization become the key components when we use LSP as a development tool.

Another dimension of LSP is its potential to generate peak performance, or "flow," which happens when people become fully involved in an activity. They become energized, focused, and enjoy what they are doing. The LSP method can enable this fantastic experience of flow, which makes it very effective and efficient in work situations.

Storytelling and metaphors are important dimensions of play and LSP because they are integral parts of the human experience. As we touched upon in the previous chapter, within organizations, stories play a role when contributing to the development, understanding, and transformation of the beliefs and values of the organization. Metaphors make storytelling livelier and more colorful. Metaphors are a form of figurative speech that describes one thing through the symbolic representation of something else to help clarify things and situations. Work communication is often filled with metaphors because it enhances shared understanding.

The Connection to the Fields of Psychology and Behavioral Science

The LSP method is built upon two complementary learning theories: constructivism[2] and constructionism.[3] According to constructivism, we produce knowledge and meaning based on what we experience, and how we actively interact with the world from childhood to adulthood. Constructionism focuses on how individuals learn. It recognizes that, when learning something, we benefit from constructing both mental and real models of what we experience. We, therefore, learn more efficiently when we build something with our hands, as it is an effective and efficient way to encourage thinking.

All LEGO materials leverage these ideas and so does the LSP method. When playing seriously, people in organizations create abstract ideas in a more concrete, visual, and tangible way.

A Facilitated Process

LSP is a facilitated process, where participants are led through a series of questions, which go deeper and deeper. Each participant builds their own three-dimensional

LEGO model in response to the facilitator's questions using specially selected LEGO bricks. These 3D models serve as the basis for group discussion, knowledge sharing, problem-solving, and decision-making. The purpose is to maximize the full potential, insight, confidence, and commitment of all the people around the table.

A key success factor for working with the LSP method is competent process facilitation. If you simply throw a bunch of LEGO bricks on the table and ask people to engage in the delicate process of serious play, you may risk intimidation. Facilitators need to create the necessary sense of psychological safety, engagement, and group cohesion, which means they need to be skilled.

In the following case study, you will hear how the LSP method can be brought into action, and after the case study, the actual facilitation guide will follow.

 CASE STUDY: STRATEGY & TRANSFORMATION STARTING UP AS A NEW POWERHOUSE

"Make-it Mine" workshop accelerated building up a strong team through empowerment

– Jakob Meiling, Senior Director, Strategy & Transformation

CONTEXT OF THE "MAKE-IT-MINE" WORKSHOP IN STRATEGY & TRANSFORMATION

The Strategy & Transformation team was a newly formed team with a new leader. It was a merger of different already existing teams consisting of 40 employees with capabilities and sub-teams within Strategy, Business Development, Transformation, and Portfolio Management.

In starting up this team, there was clear direction, investment, and priority for it to be a more end-to-end driven organization that would execute from Strategy to Transformation on the bigger strategic priorities of the LEGO Group. In this case, Meiling shares his leadership experiences with running a "Make-It-Mine" workshop, as a part of getting the team to understand the change and to engage and be empowered in the next steps of the journey:

> We discussed in the leadership team that getting the team together would make so much sense, as we did not know each other and each other's teams. We had a clear vision and direction. We created a "big picture" vision as a visualization of the vision and brought the team on board in how we saw the journey, as a metaphor of a ship following the same direction with the different sub-teams.

Vision: The powerhouse that ensures clear direction and value creation for the LEGO Group, from Strategy to Execution, being an enabler and sparring partner to the Executive Leadership Team. Visual version in Figure 6.8 on page 101.

Figure 6.8 S&T Powerhouse "Big Picture" vision visualization. Outlined by/property of cccccccc.tv.

And everything was new – that's why we arranged this off-site, which would allow us to work with the different relationships and interfaces. We wanted to empower the organization as it's a team with strong profiles and individuals, and we wanted to create a feeling of the transformation being done in collaboration with the full team and across the sub-teams. At the same time, we were humble toward getting the next steps in place with full engagement. So it was really to "DoubleClick" on the vision to prepare for the next steps and prove that we could make it happen. The objective of the session was to connect and engage the organization, and to create an understanding of the importance of working more end-to-end and across the different sub-teams to get the needed force and implementation power. At the same time, the goal was to create more awareness and understanding of the change and the reason for being in the different teams, and in this way create curiosity for people to start working together.

The objectives were to engage and empower. This was a direction that no one from the organization had influence on, so it was critical to get involvement now and co-produce the next steps. It was a clear steer that we should have something tangible and specific outcome of it as well.

The social aspect was an important part of it as well, to get people closer together and to create good and positive relations across the teams. We could have over-indexed the social dimension even more, I see now. The teams were very different – getting insights into the capabilities and reasons-for-being was super valuable for going from four separate teams to becoming one team.

Meiling explains how the LEGO Seriously concept provided a new way of communicating and collaborating:

Using the LEGO bricks to facilitate the dialogues created a common language and a common experience. It was great to have our product in our hands but, additionally, it made us all have the same starting point, as a kind of equality. We started with the skills building to get started, and everyone was building, leaning-in, and participating to the same extent.

In addition to the great dialogues and giving the teams the opportunity to reflect and explore how to take this change to the next level, and make it more tangible through dialogue on actions and new behaviors, this was definitely the first step in becoming one team. The more specific outcome of the session was that we identified what it would take to make becoming an S&T Powerhouse a reality, both at the individual, sub-team and at the full S&T level, based on a specific plan with tasks and behaviors. It was almost as if this was the glue that brought us together. An additional benefit was that we could clearly see a very strong and accelerated start on new initiatives coming up, to be solved across the sub-teams, and we actually succeeded in making smaller powerhouses across the teams, for example, on initiatives like *Route to China* and *Center of Excellence* within B2B. And I definitely see that this session was contributing to this powerful start on new initiatives and carving the way to becoming a strong S&T Powerhouse.

How to Bring It into Action?

In the following, you will find an example of a facilitated LSP process targeted to a Make-It-Mine session in the same approach that was deployed in Meiling's S&T session. The session consists first of a skills-building section followed by deeper questions to be built through LEGO models.

Activity 2: Make-It-Mine "Building Your Change Journey"

Purpose	Content
Introduction **Overview of LSP**	Welcome to the workshop – and emphasize the objectives: • To internalize the aspirations for the S&T Team through the use of LEGO Serious Play. • To get the LEGO product in our hands. • To create concrete and tangible examples and elements of the change journey toward fulfilling our "S&T Reason for Being."

	Walk through the agenda of the session: 1. Warming up/introduction exercises. 2. Part I – each team is building their own interpretation of the S&T Reason for Being. 3. Part II – Connecting the dots in the S&T Powerhouse with key focus on building the integrators/connectors between teams.
Introduce LSP **What is LSP?**	Highlight that LEGO Serious Play is: • A method used for working with communication, strategy development, and team development. • A method that uses LEGO elements to build stories about our world, both the tangible and the intangible. • Based on the concept of our "hand-knowledge." Explain that you can use the LEGO bricks in two different ways, you can build a car and you can build a house. Both models are from the tangible world, and you will try to build it in a way that looks as much as possible like the real world. In LSP, you build models to tell stories from the intangible world. It could be about a team and collaboration. If you build gears into a crane it has one meaning – and if you build gears into a model being about team collaboration, it has another meaning. So LSP is a method where you use bricks to tell stories about team life, culture, and things that you cannot really touch or feel. This is the very short version of LSP. We know that we know more than we know. And by using our hands to build and construct, we are activating our brain and our subconsciousness in a different way where our hands can support building what we think. Wrap up the introduction by explaining that LSP was developed in 1994 by the owner of the LEGO Group, Kjeld Kirk Kristiansen to destruct "leaning backwards" meetings. In his leadership team he wanted more "leaning forward" meetings with higher activity and group dynamics. In traditional meetings, 20% of the participants talk 80% of the time. There is a tendency that these 20% are very focused on what they are going to say next – that is how "leaning backwards" meetings are created. The rest of the group feels that they are not being heard or don't feel that they are part of the meeting. LSP was made to disrupt this kind of meeting. These traditional kinds of meetings may be good when you just have to inform people (e.g., information meetings), but sometimes we need meetings where more group activity and dynamics are created.

Skills building introduction	**Everyone can build and share**
	Introduce the first building exercise – following instructions. Here a standard LSP starter kit was used.[4]
	Brief the team that they should:
	Build a model following the instruction:
	• Build individually.
	• Build one of the models from the instruction.
	• If you finish, you can build one more model (do not take the first model apart).
	• It is not a competition.
	Modify the model to show: "What energizes me in my job?"
Skills building part II	**What energizes me in my job?**
	Introduce the next exercise:
	• Take the model you built from instruction – play with your model and use it to find out what you like about working in the S&T Team – what is energizing you?
	• Make a little story about one of the things.
	• Adjust your model if needed.
	• You have 3–4 minutes – individually – no talking.
	• Share at the team tables.
First model building	**The change right now**
	Introduce the next exercise – and explain that you will ask a question, and they build the answer.
	1. The change situation right now?
	Build one model that you feel characterizes the change right now or one aspect (top of mind issue) of the change right now. It can be something tangible or intangible, such as new colleagues, new tasks, or a new role.
	Share your model.
Change aspiration at sub-team level	**What does success look like for us when the change is completed?**
	• Realistic vision 6 months from now; how we want the nature and character of the outcome of the change?
	1. Build a model that tells the story about how you would like the nature, spirit, and character of the outcome of change to be 6 months from today – when we meet in 6 months (temperature checkpoint). What do we do and how do we achieve this? (6 min).
	From now on, your models should not be taken apart. Provide some specific and relevant examples that participants can relate to. Share in sub-teams:
	2. Share the story of your models at the tables.
	3. Everyone asks clarifying questions and what is absolutely critical about your model.
	4. Mark with the red brick the most important element of your model.

The S&T story	**What does success look like for us?** 1. Share the story of your models at the sharing tables in the sub-team. 2. Create the story for the sub-team – and bring the models in formation so they are linked – so the formation itself ties the individual stories together in a power team story in 6 months. Add links and connectors. 3. How can you tell the story in 2 min to the full S&T team? – practice the story (more people should be able to tell the story). 4. Ask if everybody is happy with the formation – if someone is not satisfied, further positioning is needed. 5. Make sure that everyone has the same version of the story – the core meaning of the story should be the same. 6. Make sure that at least two team members can tell the story. 7. Tell and share the story with the full team. Sub-teams tell stories – taking turns, visiting the different sub-team tables, and listening/recording the stories. Let each one build what they will focus on specifically in the aspiration. Make sure you don't go into how we do it, but instead focus on the end-state. What does it look like in our hopes? Full LSP landscape kit and identity kits are brought into play.
Change aspiration at S&T Level	**Connecting the dots in the S&T Power House** 1. Bring the team models to the big sharing table. 2. Based on team stories you have heard – where do you see the connections? Add links and connectors from your model (10 min). 3. Share where you see the most important connection. 4. Connections are bringing us forward toward fulfillment of our aspiration – creating synergies.
Issues we need to address (concentric circles)	**Opportunities and challenges to reach the aspiration** Build the issues we need to address/deal with in regard to achieving and being successful in/with reaching the aspiration. This can be both opportunities and challenges. 1. Share the story of your model. 2. Place your model in concentric circles (must take action on, good to take action on, nice to take action on) and group issues within the same topic. 3. Add names to the different actions. Build a model of something you see as issues we need to address/deal with in this change situation in order to be successful. Opportunities to be built on green plates – challenges on grey plates. Most impactful issues to be placed closest to the aspirational model – agreed upon by dialogue and by participants moving issues around (be respectful to the participants' own models – they know what they have built and the intent behind it).

The future behavior	1. What are you going to do about it? Build at least one model of how it is going to manifest in your behavior (don't build what you want, build the *behavior* you want and how you will see it).
	2. Share your story.
	Keep the aspirational model. Some of you actually can do it in 6 months, so how is this going to manifest in your behavior?
Placing responsibility	Promoting the behavior and giving feedback or asking for feedback. It does not have to be your own model if you feel more strongly for another one. You can also put more models together if you want to be responsible for more than one.
	The connection could also be one of the challenges – the connections are important.
	Materials: connectors (18–20 strings).
	Take pictures of the models with small text cards, or map out the key actions/behaviors and responsibilities on flip charts.
Wrap-up	General follow-up and closing.

In the following activities, you will find inspiration on another shorter and lighter "Make-It-Mine" approach that you can bring into play – to start up the engagement and dialogues on the change.

Activity 3: Make-It-Mine and Change Campfire Inspirational Facilitation Overview

The LEGO campfire concept was originally created as part of a Leadership Initiative, called LEGO Leadership Playground. In this concept, campfires were events where "missions" or mini-experiments were set up to practice the LEGO behaviors (curiosity, bravery, and focus), and "campfires" were opportunities to get the team together to reflect on those behaviors.

Since it was created in 2019, the idea of campfires has mushroomed. It has been brought into play in sessions on diversity and inclusion, as well as other initiatives like inspirational events. And this concept has been used successfully in change contexts as well. With an existing concept like this one that the organization feels comfortable with, this has proven itself to be a great approach for reflections and dialogues.

What Is It?

A campfire is a mental or physical space for getting the team together where team members can challenge assumptions, ask questions, give feedback, and just be vulnerable. Generally, change campfire discussions are facilitated by change catalysts or leaders, or even people from the team. The team dialogue is an approach to help individuals in the team as well as the team *all together to reflect on how to take the change mission to the next level.*

Why It Matters?

The purpose is to symbolically create a safe conversation space for the team where they reflect on where to be brave, focused, and curious as well as to design missions. From a change perspective, humans are hard-wired to be suspicious of change. It's no surprise that, handled badly, change can threaten some of our most fundamental human needs. With a little consideration and the right tools, we can help our employees not only trust but embrace change and help them be agile, not fragile.

If we get this moment right, we'll get:
Explored tactics for how you and your team can help personalize the change, including reflections and dialogues on how to take their change mission to the next level:

- Further understanding of what will change
- Understand how individuals and the team feel about the change
- Prepare the team on how to contribute and get ready for the new direction

If we don't get it right:
Difficulties in understanding the change or not relating to it can result in people going in different directions rather than working together in the same direction. If we avoid engaging the teams and don't create a safe space for dialogue and reflection, this could result in feelings of being excluded from and not being part of the change journey. To a certain level, we need people to be part of the change and to be empowered to make the change happen in their daily work.

How to Bring It into Action?

Change Campfires can be run physically or virtually. They can happen as part of an existing team meeting so long as the facilitator has been clearly communicating and setting up expected behaviors to be seen as part of a campfire conversation. Here, you'll find an example of how a change campfire can be facilitated.

Activity 3: Make-It-Mine Inspirational Facilitation Guide "Change Campfire"

Purpose	Content
Welcome, introduction, and walk-through key changes	Welcome everyone to the sessions – thank them for prioritizing/participating. Highlight that over the next hour, we'll work on our understanding of the change and how we as a team can succeed – and what it will take to feel open to change going forward. Explain the session will consist of two parts: 1. Understanding the change 2. How to prepare myself and to contribute to this now Start with a walk-through of the key changes for the team based on townhall presentation, or email, or one-pagers explaining the key changes or change story. Let me start by sharing, e.g., leader change story.
Part 1 **Understanding the change**	Ask all participants to take 5 minutes and reflect individually on questions 1–3 in the first sections – write the questions in the chat or on a slide. • What do I understand about the change? What will change? What will be different? • What do I think and how do I feel about the change? • What do I like about the change and what do I not like about the change? • What questions do I have? Ask to share key reflections from participants – encourage them to share instead of bringing them unwillingly into the spotlight, "Who would like to share...?"
Part 2 **How to prepare and contribute?**	This is the same approach as in the first part: • How can I prepare myself? How can I contribute in the best way now? • How can I contribute to support the change? Consider using the Leadership Playground Behaviors (focus, be brave, be curious) • What support do I need to succeed? Ask all participants to take 5 min and reflect individually on questions – write the questions in the chat or on a slide.

Part 3 My change map	Here you can include the "My change map" exercise (described in Activity 1) which will wrap up the session in a nice way. At the same time, it will connect nicely with follow-ups on the session, for example, through one-to-one meetings with leaders or peers. You will find the facilitation guide in the Make-it-Mine session 1 in this chapter.
Wrap-up of session and next steps	Explain the highlights from the session: • A general understanding of how we as a team will be impacted • Understand how I feel about the change and how ready I am for the change – and how to succeed Ask if there are any questions based on the session. Explain the next steps: e.g., new team session, open dialogue session, etc. Thank the participants for their time and their active participation.

Activity 4: Building and Maintaining Personal Resilience

In times of change resilience is crucial. Resilience is seen as the speed and strength of your response to adversity. When you encounter a difficulty, a hardship, or a challenge, how quickly and how effectively are you able to marshal the strength to either overcome that challenge or persevere in the face of it.

What Is It?

Personal resilience is a critical skill for success through the ability to adapt well in the face of adversity, challenges, and opportunities. This session will provide inspiration and tactics on how to thrive, rather than just survive, in a time of uncertainty and ambiguity.

Why It Matters?

It is important in times of change to understand that resilience is not an unlimited resource, but rather something you need to build and maintain. In this session, you will get more clarity on how you can build resilience and what works for you. This builds strength and ability to connect to the new world, and also helps to bounce back and feel more secure which will leverage performance and can have a positive impact on others.

If we get this moment right, we'll get:

Understanding of how you can build up resilience, a process that many people are not aware of, and how to be prepared in order to steer yourself in a resilient way, leading and supporting others in the change. Additionally, it will lead you to consider your own mindset, well-being, and readiness to embark on a specific change journey.

If we don't get it right:
If you lack resilience, you will find it difficult to navigate the change. The most troubling characteristic of low resilience is the lack of hope or vision for the future. It could also result in finding yourself dwelling on problems, feeling victimized, and becoming overwhelmed and uncertain, all of which will influence the way you are leading the change.

How to Bring It into Action?

A session on how to build and maintain personal resilience can be run both live and virtually. It can be experienced as a major topic and many people will first need to understand what personal resilience actually is. People can start by reflecting and working with their own tactics on how to build their own personal resilience. Providing some pre-work/reading and asking people to prepare their thoughts on the topic ahead of time can be valuable. It can also be run as a partial self-study followed by bringing some of the exercises into play in the session.

Activity 4: Building and Maintaining Personal Resilience Inspirational Facilitation Overview

Introduction	**Personal Resilience** **Key point** To help get you in the right mindset and to help navigate yourself and lead others in the change. Additionally, to consider your own mindset, well-being, and readiness to embark on a specific change journey. The key objective is to provide you with: 1. An understanding of what personal resilience is. 2. Tips and tools and an opportunity to come up for air from the daily demands of getting things done. 3. An opportunity to work on your own examples of how to build your personal resilience. If the target group of your session is people leaders, emphasize that, as a leader, they will play a critical role in leading others in the change. Great leaders demonstrate emotional intelligence behaviors such as empathy, integrity, humility, and self-awareness with the ability to motivate and engage. Emphasize that we are all really busy getting things done, so much so that we at times rely on muscle memory or autopilot mode to the extent that we even don't know if we are standing on our heads instead of our feet. The time you spend here is to offer the opportunity to pause and to move from the unconscious or autopilot state to reflection. You can call it "tuning in" with the goal of achieving full consciousness where you become more aware of your thoughts, words, and actions. And you can make deliberate choices toward inspired action. Highlight that to begin to appreciate your current state of personal resilience, it is probably helpful to understand what resilience means. Defining resilience can help you recognize it.

What is resilience?	Resilience is defined as becoming strong and flexible – to thrive rather than just survive in a time of uncertainty and ambiguity. It is about learning to grow rather than to crumble in the face of adversity. The common definition is the ability to be flexible and grow when being pulled and stretched. Resilience enables us to face challenges and opportunities in a way that builds muscles and strength to succeed while extracting and applying lessons from previous experiences. To share an example sourced from LEGO history, a quote from the founder Ole Kirk Kristiansen during the crisis in 1932: "Although the economic crisis brings tough times, misfortune is sometimes great." Ole Kirk Kristiansen managed to retain his positive approach – and his sense of humor. So instead of crumbling in the face of adversity, Ole saw new possibilities, which generated enthusiasm to move forward.
Why is it important?	**Why is resilience so important?** • It gives us the strength and ability to adapt to rapidly changing conditions and helps us to be more open to try new approaches, feel more secure, and acknowledge mistakes and learn from them to move forward. Resilient people tend to have more energy and focus and reflect a can-do attitude. These traits can enhance performance and can have a positive impact on others. Although some people seem to be born with more resilience than others, you can learn how to boost and build up your own resilience. • It is important to be aware that your storage of resilience is not unlimited – you need to build/fuel it up through awareness. • The more you are feeling out of your comfort zone, the more likely it is that your own personal resilience will be lower, so it is important to recognize what behaviors might be symptomatic of you having low resilience. Having some tips and tricks to build up your personal resilience is critical in these times. In tables or pairs: Think of a time when you noticed you had low resilience or when someone else supported you and noticed you had low resilience. Be ready to share ideas/examples back in plenum – and brief based on the questions this figure. **Figure 6.9, page 112: Maintaining and building your personal resilience** Ask people to share their examples in plenary.
How to build resilience?	**How to build resilience** Explain that there are four primary dimensions of resilience: • Physical • Emotional • Cognitive • Personal Your overall well-being and effectiveness is strengthened by your ability to consider and care for each of these four dimensions.

An exercise you can do by yourself or in a group to help you maintain personal resilience (input from pre-work)

| Think of a difficult time you've been through before either in your personal or work life | What actions helped you stay resilient and move forward? | How could you apply or use these actions in this situation? |

Figure 6.9 Maintaining and building your personal resilience.

	The physical dimension can be improved through physical activities, healthy eating, and getting enough sleep. By caring for your physical well-being, you can maximize your energy and increase your capacity and productivity.
	The emotional dimension can be improved by having strong social connections and a professional network for support and the feeling of being connected to a broader community. Emotional agility and awareness enable us to demonstrate empathy, humility, and patience. A combined strong emotional dimension helps you to build and sustain positive and constructive relationships.
	The cognitive dimension is where the focus is on mindfulness. This is where we build the ability to tune in and be conscious of our thoughts and actions. When we practice mindfulness, we are able to be more in the present which helps to maintain focus for longer periods of time and sharpen our decision making.
	The personal dimension is where we get clear about our own core values, our reason for being, and to be grounded in an attitude of gratitude. How often do you take the time to reflect on how you are showing up, in the way that you relate to others, and whether they will see you in the same way that you see yourself? With clarity on this personal dimension, we are able to be much clearer on what matters most which enhances our ability to prioritize. You can share this overview.
	You can share the overview of **Figure 6.10** on page 113.
POS approach	There is a simple approach to use when you recognize that your resilience is lower: P O S – Pause, Observe, and Solve. The trick is to take a step back and observe the situation. Reflect on what is going on around you, and shift the perspective as needed to move into productive thinking to create options and find the choices you have at this moment. Once you have considered all options, you will be better prepared to make a conscious deliberate choice toward a solution.

Physical

Maintaining physical wellbeing

- **Exercise** – physical exertion counteracts the effects of stress
- **Sleep** – Rest is critical to recovery & energy levels
- **Eat** – A healthy, balanced diet helps maintain the right fuel for your body and brain
- **Relax** – set aside time to separate yourself from work (e.g., a walk, read a book, yoga)

Emotional

Maintaining healthy social interaction and contacts

- **Maintain relationships** – invest time in those important to you
- **Use your network** – who can you talk to about concerns, ideas, & challenges?
- **Stay social** – don't withdraw from opportunities to get out and interact

Cognitive

Maintaining focus

- **Maintain focus** – invest time in what is most important to you
- **Decision making** – keep focus on taking the right decisions
- **Mindfulness** – practice mindfulness to pay attention to your awareness and reduce stress

Personal

Keep the clarity on what matters most

- **Core values** – be grounded in your core values
- **Prioritisation** – focus on what is most important right now
- **Be realistic** – define what you can/cannot control and focus your energy on the things you can affect

Figure 6.10 Maintaining and building your personal resilience, tactics.

A LEGO example	Here is an example from the LEGO history to bring this to life:
	The year is 1942 and Ole Kirk Kristiansen's toy workshop has just burnt to the ground. Obviously, he steps back and observes what remains of his life's work. Does he give up? We know that answer. So what do you think he had to do? In order to have the strength to move forward he had to shift his perspective and consider all options. The choice he made was not to give up – and the solution was to rebuild his business. Linking back to the four dimensions of resilience besides hard work and dedication, Ole Kirk Kristiansen was very clear on his purpose and mission, linking into the personal dimension. He created a strong network of family and friends to help him through the tough times, coming from the emotional dimension. Additionally, this required his energy and capacity to see it through – linking to the physical dimension.
	In the spirit of moving from an unconscious, autopilot state to conscious and deliberate action, let's take a few moments to reflect on some key questions, turn your attention inwards, and consider the following based on the dialogue and your reflections so far in the session.
	Think about a time of change in your life, it can even be right now. You might want to write the first things that pop into your head as you consider these questions: • Am I aware? When am I feeling strong, and "in the zone"? • What are my emotional triggers? • What resources are available to me for support? • What can I draw on from past experiences? • What made me successful in navigating those experiences? • What behaviors did I observe? • What did I do differently as a result? • How do I make sure that I am okay, so I can care for and about others?
Wrap-up	**Wrap-up by connecting back to the key elements from the session** To maintain and build up your personal resilience through change consider the four dimensions of your life: **PHYSICAL, EMOTIONAL, COGNITIVE,** and **PERSONAL.** Doing this will help you keep going when things get tough. P O S – through awareness and reflection, take the time to consider all options and make conscious deliberate choices toward a solution. And finally, it is super important to recognize that you must care for yourself before you can lead others.

CASE STUDY: TRAVEL RETAIL MOVING FROM A GLOBAL, CENTRAL FUNCTION TO THE MARKET GROUPS

We were being listened to and had influence on the way forward – that made a huge difference

– Annette Rosendahl, Director, Key Account Management

CONTEXT OF THE CHANGE JOURNEY "MAKE-IT-MINE" AND "PERSONAL RESILIENCE" WORKSHOP IN TRAVEL RETAIL

The Travel Retail team had previously been a global team with accountability for the Travel Retail channel for the strategic, development, and commercial agenda. The team had grown over the years, which resulted in a bigger focus on operating globally across all regions. A change was announced where the team would have to take a more strategic approach going forward instead of the more opportunistic approach they had always taken up to this time. In that context, it was decided that the future structural setup of the team would change their business focus and, at the same time, the Travel Retail business would be moved out to the different Market Groups, no longer being a global function. The majority of the team was based in Denmark and the majority of the new roles would move to the Market Group that was already based across regions. Based on this decision, there was a need to find a way to restructure into a new business model.

Naturally, this resulted in a certain level of ambiguity in the team, and the future direction was communicated to the team from the beginning to ensure full transparency of future direction for this channel. The team appreciated the openness and that the future direction was shared so early in the process. Significantly, the team had a period of nine months where they would not know if there was a job for them in the future. This was a time of ups and downs and an intense period where they would have to deal with providing knowledge about the change while simultaneously supporting the design of the new setup, handling changes for customers in line with the LEGO "Partner Promise," and creating their own individual change journeys. The team consisted of 14 employees who were close and very proud of the business they had built up over the years. A team member expressed that they were like a small family, knowing each other well, with strong trust and caring relationships.

A global and cross-functional project team was established with Travel Retail, Legal, Tax, Finance, and Transformation specialists to support both the business and the people part of the transformation. Annette Rosendahl was part of the project team together with the leader of the team and had a senior specialist role in the Travel Retail team. With their strong channel knowledge and experience, they supported the effort to design the best future structure for Travel Retail becoming a smaller, but important and complex business area. Rosendahl expresses here how it made a difference for her to be part of the project team:

> I really appreciated having a role on the project team as it made the process easier to engage in. It was great being involved, even

though it sometimes was tough to be closer to it compared to the rest of the team. Personally, it felt as if I was not part of the decision, but I could influence and be part of designing the process and the new set-up. Leaders and the project team listened to me based on my experience and knowledge of the channel. For me it was very important and also made it possible to be part of the change as I was involved in the process very early and made the decision that I wanted to stay in this and be a key player of the transformation.

I was a part of building up the Travel Retail business, and the business and customers are very close to my heart. I wanted to make sure that the business was well anchored in the Market Groups – without knowing my own future role in it. But working through this and designing the new setup, that worked for me. In addition to my role on the project team, I also still had my operational role as Key Account Manager and had contact with customers who were not aware of the change. It was a difficult time to have more roles. I had my own change journey – and also needed to handle the change journeys of the customers. It meant that I had to prepare my own change journey ahead of the journey of the customers. That gave me time to understand, internalize and be ready for the questions I would meet in the dialogues with the customers.

Moreover, we also had to ensure that the new setup was done based on our existing knowledge and experience of the business, and the channel, to secure a setup that could work well in practice. At a certain point in time, I accepted that I could not change the decision that had been taken. Neither could I influence how I would be impacted as an individual. But I had influence and could ensure that everything we had built over the years was deployed in the best possible way to maintain the future of the business we had worked so hard to build. That was my contribution. Our team's concern was that if the business was split into very small units, the focus over the years would disappear.

In order to get ahead and be proactive, we started up the sales team, brainstorming on what we thought the future state could look like. That provided me with an assurance that it was not only the way I saw the future but also in line with the knowledge and thinking of my peers – each of us representing different regions. It gave me a certain level of confidence that I was not only speaking for myself but on behalf of the rest of the sales team – and how we saw this channel in the future. This involvement also created a level of calmness in the team.

This transformation was handled a bit differently than previous changes like it, as our team was informed about the change in the early stages. And that was quite interesting when we were in the last and final team session and all that clarity on how we would be impacted came out. We were all out of energy, despite the fact that the majority of the team was so happy ending where we did. But everyone appreciated the openness in the process and the trust we were given, despite it being super exhausting. Getting the information so early (we were not aware that it would drag out that long) made it sometimes difficult to go to work. Some days were better than others. As a team, we were great in supporting each other. I am not sure that I have experienced such a supportive team before.

We were all going through different emotions in our journey: anxiety, anger, sadness, some wanted to give up, and others ignored it and tried to pretend that it was not happening. But we were good at accepting that we as individuals had different reactions, and were in different places in our journeys. We supported each other when we needed it. If people were struggling with seeing the future or doubting their own resources and competencies, then all of these emotional reactions were put into play here. This is because we did not know what the future structure would look like. We were doubly worried, on behalf of the business but also on behalf of ourselves as we did not know how we would be impacted as individuals. And we made several loops in the change journey – being on a good path, but then looping back. And everyone's reactions were very different and individual.

Acknowledging that this was a tough, but very important, few months for this business area, several change activities were planned for the team to make them feel confident despite the uncertainty. The company depended on the team delivering the daily operations while, at the same time, handling the changes toward the business in a professional way. The approach was to ensure a high level of engagement from the senior leader of the area – to be very clear on making the case for change directly to the team and why. So the first step was to setup an engagement session with the senior leader meeting with the team to explain the Change Vision while allowing people to ask questions and share reflections. Most importantly, it was to listen to and engage with the team.

In the overview below (Figure 6.11, page 121) you will see the process used for the timeline/key milestone overview and the content of the different change activities for the team. This also served as a monthly status update to our senior stakeholders.

In the "Make-It-Mine" session, we included the different elements as you can see above. The overall objective was to provide the team with knowledge and tools to help them to navigate the change. They got insights into emotional reactions and had a team dialogue based on their emotions at that moment – and also their motivational styles. Another key element was tactics for building personal resilience and getting them started on their change maps that they could use in continued and follow-up dialogues with their leader.

Rosendahl explains here how she experienced the session and her key takeaways:

In the change session, I sensed that we were directed in a way that we should take ownership of the change, both exploring how we would handle it and what we would like our legacy to be. Those two elements were my key takeaways.

In general, it was great to be part of a team where we had such a psychologically safe space, where we dared to share everything and all our emotions. Nobody was protective around their own career, or protective of themselves personally. It felt like we were a family, in a way, where those outside of this team could not understand how we were feeling. And I think that this actually helped the team to let off steam and have an outlet for emotional things. And that helped us to focus on the business and daily operations.

We got great feedback from stakeholders and people close to us on how dedicated and focused we were in the whole process – to do our jobs and daily tasks. We also get some clear direction from our leader to focus on the daily operations. It was extremely valuable for us to have such a strong, empathic people leader in this situation, and we sensed very early in the process that it was important for him to transition and land the team in the best way possible. The feeling of having our leader working hard for our future and doing their best to find new roles for us made us feel even more comfortable.

In the team, there were three colleagues who had been in a similar situation before. Based on their earlier experiences, there was disbelief and skepticism toward the process and the People Promise[5] as they did not get much support before. In the session with the senior leader, when the Change Consultant from Strategy and Transformation was participating, we opened up with these three skeptics to share with them the support we could see would make a difference. In the beginning, it was important to be listened to and to be able to share concerns and thoughts. But also, at a certain point in time, we needed to draw the line and then look forward to avoid getting stuck in too many thoughts and concerns.

I still recall the first meeting we had with the senior leader of the area, where I offered the team session on career aspirations early in the process, instead of the normal process of offering this after people were laid off. By doing this proactively, we could be ready to apply for other jobs in the company in line with other internal and external candidates. And we really felt that we were being listened to and that our input was considered and taken seriously. Furthermore, it was fully adapted to our situation and context, so it became a development session and not an outplacement session. And no matter what our next steps were from a career perspective, it was super useful. We actually felt like we were doing something active and with value in the time we were waiting for further clarification.

There was a very good flow from the first Make-It-Mine session, where we had some good discussions on taking ownership of the change and our own development and which role I would take. It created more awareness of my next steps and my journey ahead. When you are in a situation like this you get influenced and impacted by the people around you, who were all in different stages of their change journeys. What was important for me was to find out where I was in my journey and what I wanted to do because we are very different as individuals.

As part of the session, we worked on our personal resilience which was a great exercise. Often you think about private and work aspects in separate ways, but for me it became clear that I could emotionally compare this work situation with a personal situation I experienced when my mother got cancer. Even though they were two very different things, I could recognize the same feelings, the feeling of helplessness and powerlessness, and the inability to influence the situation. That was the same feeling. How do I handle that? I was going through many different emotions and trying to figure out how to cope with this situation. Thoughts like how to accept that this is now part of our lives – even though it seemed very unfair and unreasonable. Which role should I take in this and what can I do to support it? I related first to how to get rid of my anger or what do I do if I cannot see the light at the end of the tunnel and the possibilities in this.

It was some of those things that I started to relate to when my mother was sick. In the change session, I shared with the team that one day when I was feeling angry with the whole work situation, I went out on an early Sunday morning with my dog and I was shouting and yelling. It was like I got rid of my anger and frustration. It just came out and I was feeling so much better afterward. It may sound like a stupid thing, but it felt as if issues and emotions piled up inside me and were suppressed, and that helped me to get it out and to move on.

And I know now that I built up my resilience by taking some long walks with my dog and listening to nature, and crying, if that was what I needed to do. This has helped me in the process of staying robust – to get out in nature and be physical and allow myself to reflect just on my own. So this exercise was an eye-opener of what works for me and this created more self-awareness on how I can build up my personal resilience and take care of myself.

When I am busy and stretched, I have a tendency to just move at full speed ahead, but I found out that when I pause and allow myself to take care of myself, that gives me more energy and robustness. When things become overwhelming and I am feeling stretched, it is valuable and important to be aware of what is working for me. In the dialogue and the sharing with the team, it became clear that we build resilience in very different ways. I build my resilience in my own company and with myself, doing yoga and taking long walks, where others needed more of the social dimension, getting energy by being together with other people to talk and have good times together. My key takeaway was that it is more about learning what is working for you and getting a better self-awareness, to find ways to generate positive energy and thoughts instead of getting into a negative spiral.

In the session, we also worked on our individual Change Maps[6] and how we take our journey. That was another eye-opener for me. Questions like "What is your role?" and "What would I like to achieve?" and "How will I influence this?" forced me to consider whether I wanted to try working for another company. If/when should I start applying for something else, if I wanted to? All the elements and reflections brought more clarity for me as the questions initiated a dialogue with myself about my future direction. I used it to consider and reflect on my way forward, and to take some deliberate choices, and I came to the conclusion that I wanted to stay and continue to work for the LEGO Group if possible, and also in the same channel, if possible. So I took the decision to stay on with the hope for a new role, whereas others did not have the patience and didn't want to stay on and wait, and they started applying for other jobs. I ended up starting in a new team with a new, exciting role. And the work on my change journey was meaningful and a great warm-up for the new role as well. What I learned in the different sessions and the awareness was something that I also could use on my way forward. It became part of my personal development to leverage my self-awareness.

So, all in all, it made a huge difference for me, that even though we could not get any job safety or assurance about our future work, we were being listened to and the change tactics and tools we asked for were provided together with additional tactics. Furthermore, we were empowered to support and give input to the new business model, and it was recognized from leaders and senior stakeholders that it was a tough situation we were in. Here, we really felt and experienced our People Promise coming through.

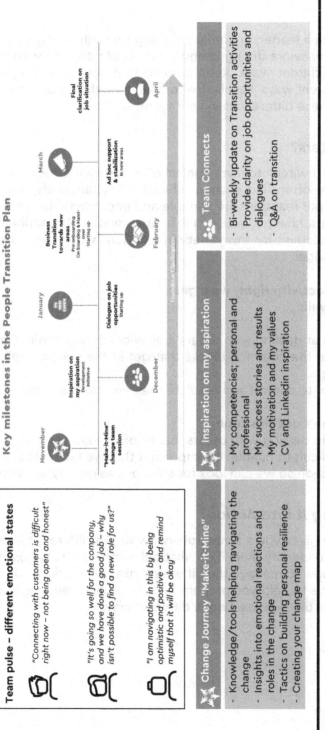

Figure 6.11 A status review of the "People & Change" approach (example).

Managing Emotional Reactions

What Is It?

Whether you're a leader, or someone going through change, you will be dealing with others' behaviors during change. As people engage with the change, they will react in different ways. Keep in mind that you, therefore, need to manage people in different ways. Familiarize yourself with the guidance in this tool to help you manage these differences in your team.

Why It Matters?

We are all "hard-wired" to favor control over our environment and circumstances. This is why we often find change difficult. Simultaneously, we are all different, and therefore our reactions are variable and unpredictable. When engaging with people during a change, you might face a variety of emotional reactions. It is important to account for this variety in reactions when trying to help your team navigate a change.

If we get this activity right, we'll get:
Leaders who will:

- Be better at dealing with others' behaviors during conflict and change.
- Recognize the common blocks that get in the way, as well as how to overcome them.
- Learn how to control and regulate their emotions in times of change.

What if we don't use this tool:
When we avoid dealing with others' behaviors, the issues can grow and become even more difficult to handle. It's important that we face disagreements or tough decisions head-on so we can look for solutions as quickly as possible.

How to Bring It into Action?

This approach gives you a simple overview of the different types of reactions to change, how to identify them (i.e., what behaviors you will see), and then provides guidance on how to manage the different types of reactions. On a practical level, you can use this to help you prepare for one-on-one sessions or discussions with team members that are reacting in different ways.

Managing Emotional Reactions Inspirational Facilitation Overview

Introduction: Emotional reactions	Introduction key point:
	Welcome and introduce today's topic on emotional reactions to change.
	Points to explain:
	As a leader you will have to deal with your team's emotional reactions which may not be what you expected from them.
	We all respond differently to change around us – some people feel intrigued and energized, whereas others feel overwhelmed and suspicious.
	When change is about to happen, we either respond positively and accept it, or negatively and reject it.
	Negative responses happen when we believe there is some kind of threat to us or there is a mismatch of resources, ability, or control to meet the change.
	In these situations, it's important that we understand the individual's perspective, so we are better placed to help people cope with uncertainty and perceived threats.
	Figure 6.12 Why can change be challenging?
	Explain:
	Let's dive into the biology and psychology for a moment.
	Why is change so hard? We are all different and complex and therefore our reactions are unpredictable.

○ We are 'hard-wired' to favour control over our environment and circumstances

○ Control = less danger = greater chances of survival

○ In a steady state, we know what we have to do to be successful

○ When things change, our control and security is threatened

Figure 6.12   Why can change be challenging?

	• **Changing people is hard:** Changing people is much, much more difficult – you don't just walk into a Town Hall, tell everyone they need to change, and then they walk away expecting everyone to accept that and do things differently straight away. • **Evolved for stability:** It doesn't help that we've evolved to prefer stability. • **Stability is critical to survival:** If you think back thousands of years to tribes of humans operating as hunter-gatherers, knowledge and control over your environment were critical to survival – i.e., obtaining food and avoiding predators. • **Only change if necessary:** Only when your survival was threatened or when your chances of survival were greater if you took a chance of moving elsewhere, did you willingly change your environment. • **Success in the workplace:** In the workplace, this equates to people knowing what they need to do (and how to do it) to be successful – they will only change if their success is threatened or if they see a better alternative. • **Hard at individual level:** Remember, if change is hard at the individual level, then it follows that complex organizations of hundreds or thousands of people will be even harder to drive changes into.
	We react emotionally and move to fight or flight which blocks the rational center, so we need to practice stepping out of our limbic system – using techniques like Pause–Observe–Solve (you will find more on this tactic in personal resilience in the previous section).
Our responses to change	**Key point:** To understand the science behind our reaction to change, and how we can use this in our communication and engagement. **Points to explain:** • That some people will always be more change ready than others. • Resistance to change usually comes from a feeling of threat. **Show Figure 6.13 – Needs that can be threatened.**

F Fairness
The decisions that affect me will be reasonable.

A Assurance
Whatever happens, it will be all right.

B Belief
I can succeed.

R Relationships
We'll get through this together.

I Identity
I feel valued.

C Control
There's plenty I can do.

Figure 6.13 Needs that can be threatened during change.

	Research shows that there are six specific needs that can be threatened during change: • **Fairness:** "The decisions that affect me will be reasonable." Our need to know decisions are made with our best interests in mind. • **Assurance:** "Whatever happens, it'll be all right." I feel comfortable that I can succeed and will meet the expectations. • **Belief:** "I can succeed." Our personal belief that we are equipped (or will be provided support) to succeed in the current and new circumstances. • **Relationships:** "We'll get through this together." Our need for support from others. • **Identity:** "I feel valued." Our need to feel that our individual identity as individuals is validated and valued. • **Control:** "There's plenty I can do." Our need to feel in control of the circumstances that affect us. Our brain treats these needs almost as intensely as survival instincts. Here are some examples: • A perceived threat to one's identity activates similar brain networks as a threat to one's life. • In the same way, a perceived increase in fairness activates the same reward circuitry as receiving a monetary reward.
	As change leaders, it's important that we keep these basic, primal reactions in mind when managing others during change and recognize our fundamental need for security. • Each of us is different and will care more about some things than others. But when one or more of these six areas are threatened, we move into a "threat state" and activate a "freeze, flight, or fight" response. • If our people are in this state, the chances are high that they will not engage with the change. *Facilitator tip:* *Share some of your own reactions to change in the past – not just at work, but also in your life – moving to a new house or something similar. This makes it easier to share and relate to the different reactions.* Ask participants: Based on everything we have discussed, where do you think people are experiencing the biggest threat?
	What actions can you take to support these people? • Ask participants to choose some examples to work through the model with. • Explain that you want everyone to take some time to consider what tactics they can apply to minimize the relevant threats and help their teams to become more change agile. In group session, based on the previous exercise, ask participants to take a moment of reflection to identify which single tactic they think will be most important for their team and which actions they will take to deliver this. Ask participants to share this with the group. **Show Figure 6.14 – Tactics when needs are threatened** and wrap up the input by walking through the different threats and tactics.

FABRIC	Tactics

Fairness

The decisions that affect me will be reasonable.

- Offer transparency
- Explain principles behind decisions
- Give as much as take

Assurance

Whatever happens, it'll be all right.

- Contain anxiety
- Talk in shades of grey
- Be a merchant of hope

Belief

I can succeed.

- Cultivate a growth mindset
- Show your belief in others

Relationships

We'll get through this together.

- Keep others connected
- Create a 'we're in this together' spirit
- Get people talking

Identity

I feel valued.

- Remind people of their signature strengths
- Surprise with small unexpected rewards
- Know individual motivators

Control

There's plenty I can do.

- Share ownership
- Give choices
- Differentiate what is and what isn't in control

Figure 6.14   Tactics when needs are threatened.

Different emotional reactions to change	**Managing reactions – points to explain:** • In addition to understanding the threats and the tactics, it is useful to understand how emotions can take hold of us, or the other person, at any point. • They can lead us to act in very different ways from how we previously planned. **Show Figure 6.15 Different emotional reactions to change.** • There are different kinds of reactions to change. • Consider which reaction you will meet when you are engaging with individuals in the team – or the team together.
	Show Figure 6.16 Emotional reactions – what behaviors you might see. • Encourage a dialogue – and ask participants what different reactions they are expecting from individuals. Allow time for reflection and dialogue in smaller teams/pairs.

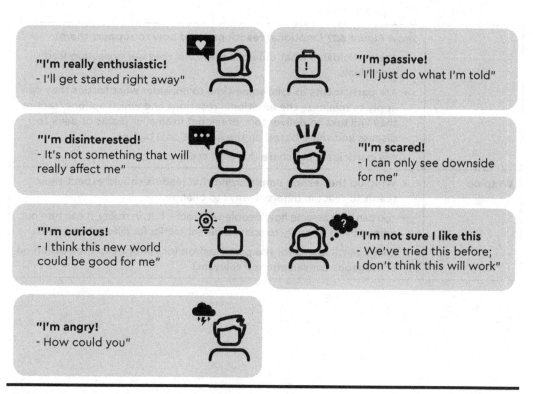

Figure 6.15 Different emotional reactions to change.

Reaction	What behaviours might you see?	How might you support someone displaying this behaviour
Curious		
Disinterested		
Thrilled		
Passive		
Scared		
Enthusiastic		
Angry		

Figure 6.16 Emotional reactions – what behaviors you might see.

	Show Figure 6.17 Emotional reactions – and how to support them? • Ask participants what different reactions they are expecting from individuals. • Ask participants to take some time to consider what tactics they can apply to minimize the emotional reactions and which actions/tactics they will take to deliver this. Break out in smaller teams or pairs to discuss and share based on the inspirational tactics • Ask participants to share this with the group.
Wrap-up	• Wrap up the session emphasizing that leaders should expect their teams to react in different ways to change. • You can only assume how people will react – but, in reality, it can turn out differently so be ready to adopt different tactics for different reactions. • Thank participants for the participation (or continue to the session on courageous conversations if relevant).

Behavior	What behaviors might you see?	How would you support them?
Curious	• Lots of questions about possibilities, next steps, how they can get involved, what it all means • Proactively exploring and finding more information • Lots of discussion and dialogue with colleagues	• 'Feed' their need for information • Encourage them to experiment and test new ways of working • Give them an active role in driving the change within your team
Disinterested	• 'Tuning out' in discussions or briefings • Not attending sessions, training or briefings for the change • Lack of engagement or questions	• Proactively bring them into the conversation – ask questions of them, seek their opinion • Help them understand how the change relates directly to their work • Emphasize how the change will benefit them personally in their role
Enthusiastic	• Visibly positive about the change and opportunities • High levels of energy to the topic • Volunteering to get involved/support the change	• Use as change agents or with an active role in leading the change in your team • Leverage energy in the project effort – if stuff needs doing to deliver the change, use these people • Challenge them (e.g., through a stretch target) to help their peers who are struggling
Passive	• Lack of action or proactivity despite seeming aligned with the change • Doing the minimum asked in relation to changes	• Proactively bring them into the conversation – ask questions of them, seek their opinion • Help them understand how the change relates directly to their work • Give them an active role in the change as a performance target
Scared	• Lots of questions about impact on roles and responsibilities • May become reserved, quiet, and visibly nervous • Potential for bursts of emotion or challenge towards what is changing	• 'Buddy-up' with those that are more confident around the change to drive peer learning • Understand the source of their concern and address it – ask "What do you need to help you feel more positive about this?" • Stay in regular, 1:1 contact – informally explore progress and their feelings about what's happening
Unsure	• Questions/comments indicating they don't believe it will work • Challenges solutions – "Why that solution? Why not this instead..?" • Questions commitment of leaders to deliver the change	• Seek ways to involve them in 'owning' the solution design or how it's rolled out/applied to the team • Provide clarity on their role in the change – and what tasks you will need their support on • Be clear on the next steps in the change – and repeat why we are doing this
Angry	• Shuts down – no engagement, questions or dialogue • Avoids the subject/anything to do with the change • Potential for bursts of anger towards the change/at briefings & dialogues	• Give them time and space to voice and share their frustrations and challenges • Try to understand the specific source of their anger and deal with it • Challenge them to get involved in the change effort so they can regain some level of control • Use the courageous conversation tool to plan a conversation if you are worried about how to engage them

Figure 6.17 Emotional reactions – and how to support them?

Courageous Conversations

What Is It?

At some point along the journey, you might be in a situation where you need to deliver a tough message or have a difficult conversation with someone. Even when we lack confidence in these situations, with the right preparation, it's possible to deliver difficult messages in the right way.

Why It Matters?

Change can be a difficult and emotional time for people. If people are impacted at an individual level, it may be necessary to have a difficult and courageous conversation with them. These conversations get more difficult when we are talking about something that's important to us. Therefore, it is important that these dialogues are handled in a way that leaders know how to control and regulate emotions that come up during these situations and dialogues. This will support both the leader and the individuals when navigating the change.

If we get this activity right, leaders will:

- Have discovered the importance of having courageous conversations – and how to frame them in a way that encourages positive outcomes, where possible.
- Learn how to control and regulate emotions during these situations and dialogues.

What if we didn't use this tool:
If we avoid having courageous conversations, the challenge can grow and become even more difficult to talk about further down the line.

How to Bring It into Action?

This workshop session can be run in a bite-sized format – and you should see the previous session on emotional reactions to change as a pre-requisite for this, as this provides a fundamental understanding of how to handle emotional reactions.

Courageous Conversations
Inspirational Facilitation Overview

Introduction	**Key points:**
	• To discover the benefits of having these difficult conversations.
	• Recognize the common blocks that get in the way, as well as how to overcome them. Learn how to control and regulate your emotions.
	• Become better able to handle others' behavior during conflict.
	Points to explain:
	• We all need to have difficult, courageous conversations at various points in our lives.
	What is a courageous conversation?
	Some examples of courageous conversations are when we need to:
	• Clear up misunderstanding.
	• Speak up and express how we think or feel about something in a difficult situation.
	• Rebuild relationships that may have become broken.
	• Confront those we work with to ensure they know what we want or don't want.
	• Deliver a difficult message, e.g., people having a new role, a new leader, being laid off, etc.
	• These conversations get more difficult if we're talking about something that's important to us, where opinions are mixed, or when we're emotionally attached to a subject.
	• We know that change can be an emotional time for people, as it can threaten some of our core "needs" (link back to needs/threats covered in Emotional Reactions to Change in the previous section).
	• Sometimes we need to communicate a difficult message. For those going through change, sometimes we feel the need to raise our concerns and give feedback to senior leaders, which can also take courage.
	• Regardless of whether you're leading others or going through it yourself, the principles of how to prepare for and have the conversation remain the same.
	Before we go into the "how," let's first think about what might stop us from having a difficult conversation. Ask participants to bring to mind a difficult conversation they had in the past, or maybe one they avoided.
	Ask them why it was difficult or why they didn't have the conversation – write thoughts on a flipchart or a virtual board.
	Share Figure 6.18: What stops us.
	Build on what you've written on the board with further examples on the slide.
	Ask participants: When you have confronted a difficult situation, and have had a courageous conversation, how did you feel afterward?

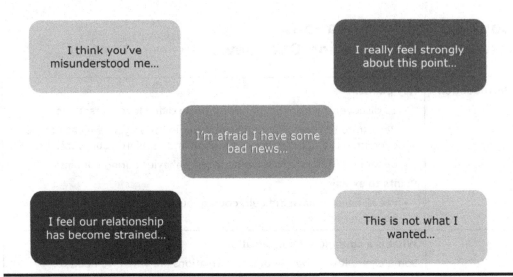

Figure 6.18   What stops us from taking the difficult dialogues?

	Share the following research:
	One study found that in the most successful and long-standing companies, those who excelled, were those who simply dealt with difficult conversations. Their ethos centered on everyone, at all levels of the business, being able to hold everyone else accountable. People took responsibility for their actions, for failure, and then for how to rethink strategies to make it better. They also found that those individuals who spoke out and were courageous were unanimously respected and listened to.
Structuring the Conversation	**Key point:** To explore how to structure and prepare for a courageous conversation and set ourselves up for success – the best possible outcome. **Share Figure 6.19: Courageous conversations – how to do it?** **Points to explain:** • There's a lot going on during a courageous conversation, so to help us get better at having them, we're going to break it down and take each element in turn. • There are three main elements to having a courageous conversation – telling our story, listening properly, and managing the reactions we get back. We can also add a fourth step in advance which is to prepare for the conversation – this is if we know we are going to be having the conversation, and it's not something we're doing "in the moment." • The cycle isn't linear – each conversation can take a different path.
	Note: As you work through each part of the structure in turn, make sure you pause to ask questions and create some space for conversation. The aim is to give participants some guidance on how to have courageous conversations – this is not a template or script they need to follow, but rather top tips. Don't dwell on any one section, unless people have questions, but aim to work through it at a steady pace.

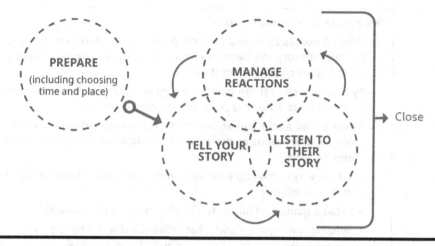

Figure 6.19 Courageous conversations – how to do it?

	Prepare – points to explain • The first part of having a difficult conversation is to prepare. Highlight that sometimes this isn't an option, for example, if we're having a conversation in the moment. However, if we do have a chance to prepare, we often prepare what we want to achieve – but to prepare fully, we need to consider not only what we want to achieve for ourselves, but also for the other person and the relationship and to think about how we can behave to make that possible. • Having the answers to these questions will help us keep on track if a conversation gets heated and will allow us to come back to what we know is important, rather than go down a side track. More often than not, when we end up in a difficult or emotionally charged conversation, we can find ourselves moving away from a dialogue and into a debate where we are just trying to "win" the argument.
	However, if we prepare properly, we can remind ourselves of why we're having the conversation, which can bring us back from unhealthy debate and into dialogue again. If you'd like to share an example of what we mean by focusing on us, the other person, and the relationship, share the following: • *What do I want to achieve?* Telling your manager you disagree with one of their change decisions/messages. • *For me:* That they hear me out and I come away understanding more about why the decision was made. • *For the other person:* To not feel accused or put on the spot (they likely weren't the one making the decision after all). • *For the relationship:* Preserve the relationship and feel like communication lines are staying open. • *How would I behave?* Approach without emotion, but with maturity and clear reasons for why I'm feeling the way I do. Demonstrating that I'm open to conversation, not closed debate.

	Tell your story – points to explain:
	
	• When it comes to having the conversation, we need to make sure we tell our full story. We need to cover the facts, how we feel about it and what bigger picture effect it has.
	
	• By taking each of these points step by step, we can build our story and give ourselves a starting point for the conversation.
	
	• As we talked about earlier, one of the reasons we sometimes avoid having a courageous conversation is because we don't really know where to start.
	
	• A simple way of making sure we convey our story is to make sure we answer the following:
	  • What's going on (linking to the change vision if relevant)?
	  • What is the impact – and what influence this will have on you?
	  • What are the next steps – e.g., follow-up dialogues?

	Ask participants: Why is it sometimes hard to express our feelings about a situation? • For example: Maybe what you are actually feeling is at odds with what you need to be communicating. Or the way that you are feeling is a result of something personal for you, that you don't want to share, but you need to find a way to communicate how it is affecting you on the whole. **Ask participants:** Why is it important to express the wider impact – and what could happen if we don't do this? • The wider impact is important because it puts your feelings into context. For example, if you're sharing a difficult message with an employee (e.g., as a result of a change they will need to relocate, or will be taking a pay cut), placing that decision within the larger change process and conversation (e.g., the wider impact) can help them to understand the rationale behind the decisions. It also helps them understand the decision isn't based on them as an individual or their performance necessarily, but rather wider strategic conversations.
	Listen to their story – points to explain: • Once we've told our "story," we need to ensure the conversation becomes a dialogue, rather than a one-sided stream of information or a debate. It can seem like quite a hard task to get the other person to open up to us and engage in the conversation, but we can do it by finding out the effect our story is having on them. We do this by listening to their story. **Ask participants** if they can think of any problems that might occur if they don't make an effort to listen to the other person.

For example:

- They won't engage with the change or the story properly and won't take on board the information and the actions.
- They can misunderstand and turn the situation into a negative (or a greater negative).

Explain that a simple way to remind ourselves to consider the other person is to make sure we get the answers to the following points:

- What do they think is going on?
- How do they feel about it?
- What do they think the wider impact is?

It's important we don't guess at or assume what they think, but actually find out by asking the right sorts of questions and really listen to their answers.

Highlight that to really listen, we need to turn off our internal filters. As humans, what we hear is channeled through filters, or we might pass judgment based on our personal opinions. What we tend to hear is often only the things that confirm our suspicions or strengthen our argument. It's for this reason that it's important we turn these filters off and put aside our argument. By asking them questions and entering into dialogue, we let the other person know that we would like their input, that we are willing to be open to suggestions, and that we care about what they have to say. This can also help to get buy-in from the other person and help them feel respected and that their opinions are being valued and heard.

Ask participants for other examples of how we can turn off our filters and tune in. For example:

- Find a quiet place so you won't be distracted.
- Turn off your phone.
- Take notes to help you focus on facts, not emotions.
- Active listening – deliberately and intently focusing and listening to every word that is said.

Share Figure 6.20: Two types of emotional responses.

- Emotions can take hold of us, or the other person, at any point of a courageous conversation, even if we've carefully planned it and are in a productive dialogue.
- They can lead us to act in a very different way from how we planned beforehand.

Managing reactions

- There are two distinct types of emotional response – the first is when either we or the other person starts to withdraw from the conversation. It may be because we or they feel unsafe or want to avoid conflict. This is called a retreat response.
- The second type is an attack response. This is when we, or the other person, start to become aggressive in getting our or their viewpoint across. It may be because we feel we are not being heard, or that we have lost control of the discussion.

EMOTIONS			
		Attack	**Retreat**
WHO	**What is it?**	Someone starts to respond aggressively or attempts to control the discussion.	Someone withdraws or avoids further conversation. Connections have been lost and barriers have been put up.
	Why does it happen?	We feel like we've lost control or we're not being heard. We're trying to persuade others to share our view	We don't feel comfortable; we want to avoid conflict; or we feel the need to protect ourselves.

Figure 6.20 Two types of emotional responses.

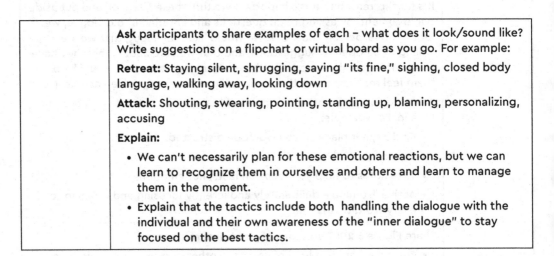

Ask participants to share examples of each – what does it look/sound like? Write suggestions on a flipchart or virtual board as you go. For example:

Retreat: Staying silent, shrugging, saying "its fine," sighing, closed body language, walking away, looking down

Attack: Shouting, swearing, pointing, standing up, blaming, personalizing, accusing

Explain:

- We can't necessarily plan for these emotional reactions, but we can learn to recognize them in ourselves and others and learn to manage them in the moment.
- Explain that the tactics include both handling the dialogue with the individual and their own awareness of the "inner dialogue" to stay focused on the best tactics.

		EMOTIONS	
		Attack	**Retreat**
WHO	**With Them**	Be generous; assume the most positive interpretation of what they say Find neutral ground Focus on what you both need to achieve	Bring them back by commenting that they seem to have retreated Dig deeper and ask questions about their thoughts and feelings Be humble and show that you don't have all the answers
	In Me (leader)	Stop trying to win Listen to what they're saying Be empathic	Be introspective; question your response Try to verbalize your thoughts Be authentic and stick to your message

Figure 6.21   How to handle emotional responses with them/in you.

	Share Figure 6.21 – How to handle emotional responses with them/in you. Depending on your group, one of the best ways to bring these reactions to life is to run a role-play getting participants to act out each of these two key responses (e.g., retreat or attack). If the leaders are going to have courageous dialogues ahead of them, it would be useful to practice one of those dialogues. Process: • Split participants into pairs. • Allow them time to think about the conversation they are going to have (if you're the manager/leader) or the reaction you are going to give (if you're the team member). • Explain that the aim of the conversation is to have the best possible discussion, preferably with some clear actions for progress. • Before you debrief, explain that we're going to run one more scenario to give everyone a chance to practice both sides of the conversation. • Ask people in their pairs to swap roles so they're now playing the opposite role from before (either Manager/Leader or Team member). • Repeat the process.
	Into action **Key point: To give participants the opportunity to prepare for and practice having a courageous conversation.** **Explain** that you've just shared a lot of information on how to structure and prepare for the conversation – now participants will have the opportunity to apply it to a conversation they are going to be having and to plan for it.

Ask participants to spend 10 minutes reflecting on an upcoming courageous conversation they need to have. If they don't have any tricky conversations coming up, ask them instead to think back on a conversation they might have had in the past, and how they might have done it differently if they'd had the chance to prepare. After 10 minutes, ask participants to turn to a partner and share two things they are going to commit to doing to ensure this courageous conversation is set up for success.

- Ask how participants felt their conversations went, for both scenarios.
- What was difficult about the reactions? If you were playing the manager/leader, how did you handle these reactions at the moment? If you were playing the team member, how did your partner's response to your reactions either help/hinder you from reaching a conclusion? Did you feel like it made you even more likely to attack/retreat?
- Ask, when you were playing the team member, what turned your reaction around? What did the manager/leader say that helped you come out of your response and work towards a solution?
- Did anyone use the tactics on the handout and, if so, to what effect?

End the role play by asking for some key takeaways from the exercise and things they feel made the biggest impact and they'll take back and use with their teams.

Wrap up the session with some key takeaways and reminders:

- Define what it is you want to achieve.
- Start with your story, when share feelings.
- Listen to their story without judgment.
- Watch out for and manage emotional responses.
- Carry out the conversation with authenticity, empathy, generosity, and humility.

Thank everyone for their participation.

TOP TIPS

- Expect your team to react in different ways.
- Adopt different strategies for different reactions, rather than a "one-size-fits-all" approach.
- Sometimes, if managed carefully and allowed involvement in the changes that affect them, people who are initially the most negative and angry can become the biggest cheerleaders.
- Beware of people who sit quietly in the middle. You often don't know what these people are thinking. At least if someone is angry, you know quickly!

SIGNS YOU'RE READY TO MOVE FORWARD...

- You know that a critical mass of people understand and embrace their role in the change.
- People are aware that change brings unexpected developments – and that you're prepared for it.

Notes

1. For more explanation on LEGO Serious Play, see videos "LSP at a Glance". https://www.youtube.com/channel/UCCq_d6dbf4XKafAwMwTNing
2. Developed by Jean Piaget (1896–1980).
3. Developed by Seymour Papert (1928–2016).
4. Starter Kit 2000414 | SERIOUS PLAY® | Buy online at the Official LEGO® Shop US.
5. You can read more about the People Promise in Chapter 1.
6. Described in Session 1 – Make-It-Mine.

CHAPTER 7

MOMENT 4 – NAVIGATING THE CHANGE

What Is It?

This is where planning meets reality, as change is being brought into daily life. The organization is rolling out a new way of working, with inevitable challenges and adaptations. This is another elastic moment, where you'll need to intervene, mainly as and when issues arise. It's also where emotional reactions will be most diverse, so there is a pressing need to get a critical mass of people into constructive, positive mindsets.

Possible signs that indicate we need help navigating the change

- People don't really know why they're doing something new
- Something doesn't work as planned – and people give up
- Change seems to be stalling, or old, unhelpful ways of working stick around

How people are feeling

- "I'm loving this – this feels genuinely fresh"
- "I'm impatient – can't we get this done more quickly?"
- "I feel guilty – I've lost some colleagues"
- "I'm disappointed – it's harder in reality than it sounded in theory"
- "I'm vindicated – this isn't perfect and I told them so"
- "I'm grieving the old way of doing things"
- "I'm overwhelmed – can't we slow down?"
- "I'm out – this is not for me"

DOI: 10.4324/9781003243113-7

Why It Matters?

If we get this moment right, we'll get:

- Renewed trust
- Continuous improvement from day one
- Shared ownership for resolving challenges
- Success stories emerging and going viral

If we don't get it right:

- Leaders lose credibility
- Cynicism spreads
- Change stalls or goes in reverse

WHERE AND HOW CAN YOU HAVE THE BIGGEST IMPACT?

In this section, you will find impactful activities and interventions to bring into play if issues, uncertainty, and emotional reactions are surfacing. You will also find methods to follow if the new ways of working are not rolling out as expected, and be ready with corrective actions and improvements where needed. Additionally, it makes a lot of sense to revisit the previous chapter on emotional reactions to change and keep this in mind as people are navigating the change. This is often when those reactions come up. For leaders to really lead the change and focus on interventions and solving the problems in the real world is "What makes a good change leader" so very important.

Where	How
Help leaders provide regular reinforcement of what needs to be done – and ensure focus on change leadership characteristics.	**What Makes a Good Change Leader page 141**
Encourage honesty and uncover current change experiences by getting among the teams and using feedback loops.	**Change Learning Groups page 147**

What Makes a Good Change Leader?

What Is It?

Creating awareness among leaders on what good change leadership looks like and what the key characters of good change leadership are.

Why It Matters?

Leaders are playing a vital role in providing encouragement and helping to iden-tify opportunities in the new ways of working and, at the same time, they are setting a clear direction. Simply being interested and supportive while engaging with people is important – and also intervening where needed.

How to Bring It into Action?

In this following guide you will get some inspiration on how to create awareness of what good change leadership looks like. This session can be combined with any other activities – and it is providing a good direction of what is needed from a change leader perspective that leaders are always very interested in.

"What Makes a Good Change Leader" Inspirational Facilitation Overview

What makes a good change leader	**Key point: To introduce the topic and ensure participants understand what good change leadership looks like.** Explain: So before we start to explore change leadership in a little more detail, let's hear your perspective on what good looks like. First encourage individual reflections: *Think about your personal experience of going through difficult changes at work either as a leader or as an individual being impacted by changes.* In pairs: *What would you single out as the key element of good change leadership?*
	Ask participants to share examples of when they experienced good change leadership – capture on a whiteboard/flip chart. Thank them for sharing. Explain that research has been done collecting the best practices of what key characteristics of good change leaders are. This is not introducing a new leadership model – this is just a representation of the key defining characteristics of good change leadership. And these are the themes that emerge as the most important. Share Figure 7.1 – and unfold/explain the different characteristics.
	This is not about traditional "comms," although that is a part of it – it's about setting up a regular dialogue so you can have your "finger on the pulse" of your teams.

Confront resistance & resolve conflict

ACTION:

1. Tackle the big issues head on
2. Prepare for the difficult dialogues and cover these off first, not last!

Don't avoid the tough conversations
Resolve roadblocks

Be humble

ACTION:

1. Don't be hard on yourself – you will make mistakes but we're all human
2. Involve your teams early in helping to build the change or problem solve

Accept you don't have all the answers –but your teams might.
Mistakes will be made –but that's ok!

Visible & accessible

ACTION:

1. Increase physical and virtual presence
2. Make it clear that people can reach out to you

Don't hide
Door is always open
Front up to the big challenges
Create a sense of 'in this together'

Walk the talk

ACTION:

1. Take a moment to reflect: "How do I need to change?", "What would demonstrate that I support this change?"
2. Don't say anything you can't back up with action

Recognize that change starts at home
Actions match words
Lead by example

Listen & share

ACTION:

1. Communicate, communicate, communicate – too much is not enough
2. Seek views and feedback from your team

Communicate frequently
Share available information
Be honest about what is/is not known
Seek regular feedback

Play the long game & win the short game

ACTION:

1. Define and continually emphasize the 'north star' or vision
2. Help people understand what they can do today and pursue these small gains – revisit (e.g., monthly)

Set a clear and compelling vision
Focus on the tangible steps in the here and now on the journey (inch by inch)

Figure 7.1 Key characteristics of good change leaders.

There are different tactics that can be used:

- **Talking cure:** Example – Psychotherapy used to be known as the "talking cure" as longitudinal studies showed equivalent recovery and improvement rates by just talking about problems.
- **Bottling of emotions:** When you are angry or frustrated, think about how much worse you feel when you keep that bottled inside.
- **Causes of stress:** This type of stress has been shown to contribute to poor physical health and definitely translates into poor performance and discretionary effort at work.
- **Stand-up meetings:** Leaders have open-door/stand-up coffee sessions with no agenda – just for people to discuss, share, and engage – and this works brilliantly.

Listen and Share

Visible and Accessible

- By knowing that you are there or seeing you, your people will have more confidence that you have them in mind.
- **Not visible = doesn't care:** prolonged absence and lack of contact give the impression that you are not concerned with their well-being.
- **Examples:** Commit to emailing back within 2 days, don't reschedule 1:1s, etc.

Confront Resistance and Resolve Conflict

- Resistance needs to be reframed more positively – it demonstrates that people are at least engaging with the change and what it means.
- All resistance has a root cause; the key is to understand and work with it – people rarely resist for no reason or just to be belligerent.
- **Kicking the can down the road:** Avoiding resistance basically kicks the can down the road – except when you see it again, it's much bigger, heavier, and scarier.

Play the Long Game, Win the Short

- This is about creating a vision of the final destination while keeping focused on the small steps going in the right direction from today.
- **Sense of direction:** In simple terms, people often need a sense of where they are going and why this is compelling – a clear vision and direction.
- **Doesn't have to be detailed:** This doesn't need to have significant detail, it just needs to be an articulation of the future state.
- **Clear, compelling, aligned:** Visions must be clear, aligned, and engaging – not full of facts and dry figures.
- **Ambiguity:** To help navigate ambiguity on the long journey, you need to give clear focus for each step of the way – e.g., deliver the "business as usual" and help translate what the individuals/team can do today.
- **Set the direction then focus on the buoys:** The best way to manage ambiguity is to set the direction in the distance but then focus people on the 10–20 buoys that mark each step.
- Example: Road trip: If I drive X to Y, I know where I want to get to and when, but I must check my route each day rather than plan everything ahead of time.
- They then set day-to-day routines and roles.

	Walk the Talk • Role modeling is a critical factor in driving organizational behavior change. • People will immediately pick up on any incongruence between what you say and what you do. • **Body language** – If I'm talking to you about something, what makes the biggest difference, my words, my tone, or my body language? There are lots of studies to support body language. **Humble** • Nobody has ever led an error-free change or transformation. • **Scars:** Anyone that's led through lots of change has plenty of scars to show for it! • **Accept that things will be tough:** Accepting that things will be tough and that mistakes are OK is a good start. • **Involve others:** Involving others early in problem solving is a great way of (1) accepting you don't have all the answers and (2) engaging people in the change effort. • **Drives buy in:** As soon as people get a chance to build the bridge, they are more likely to act as activists and supporters, so empower people as soon as you can and accept that you do not have all the answers	
Identify your strength and blind spots	**Key point: To have leaders reflect on where to focus and strengthen their change leadership** Explain: To be authentic as a leader is important as well, so "be yourself." The reason is that: • **Spot a fake:** People can spot a fake a mile away – if you try to be someone you're not, your teams will notice and you'll also be setting yourself up for a fall. • **Consistent:** Be consistent regardless of the situation. • **Human side:** Demonstrate a human side – empathy – put yourself in the shoes of your people. • **Own voice:** Speak with your own voice using your own experiences and examples – people will recognize you are being genuine and will engage more. • **Acknowledge your pluses and minuses:** Understand what you are strong at versus your blind spots and work around them. Show or hand out Figure 7.2. Brief the participants on the exercise to reflect on their strengths and their development areas. This can either be done individually or in pairs. **Ask participants to share examples of blind spots and how they will work on this.**	
Wrap-up	Close the session by mentioning some of the highlights from the session based on the specific examples that were discussed and emphasize that the good news is that most of this is not "unlearnable" or an innate skill. With some focus and effort you can tick all the boxes.	

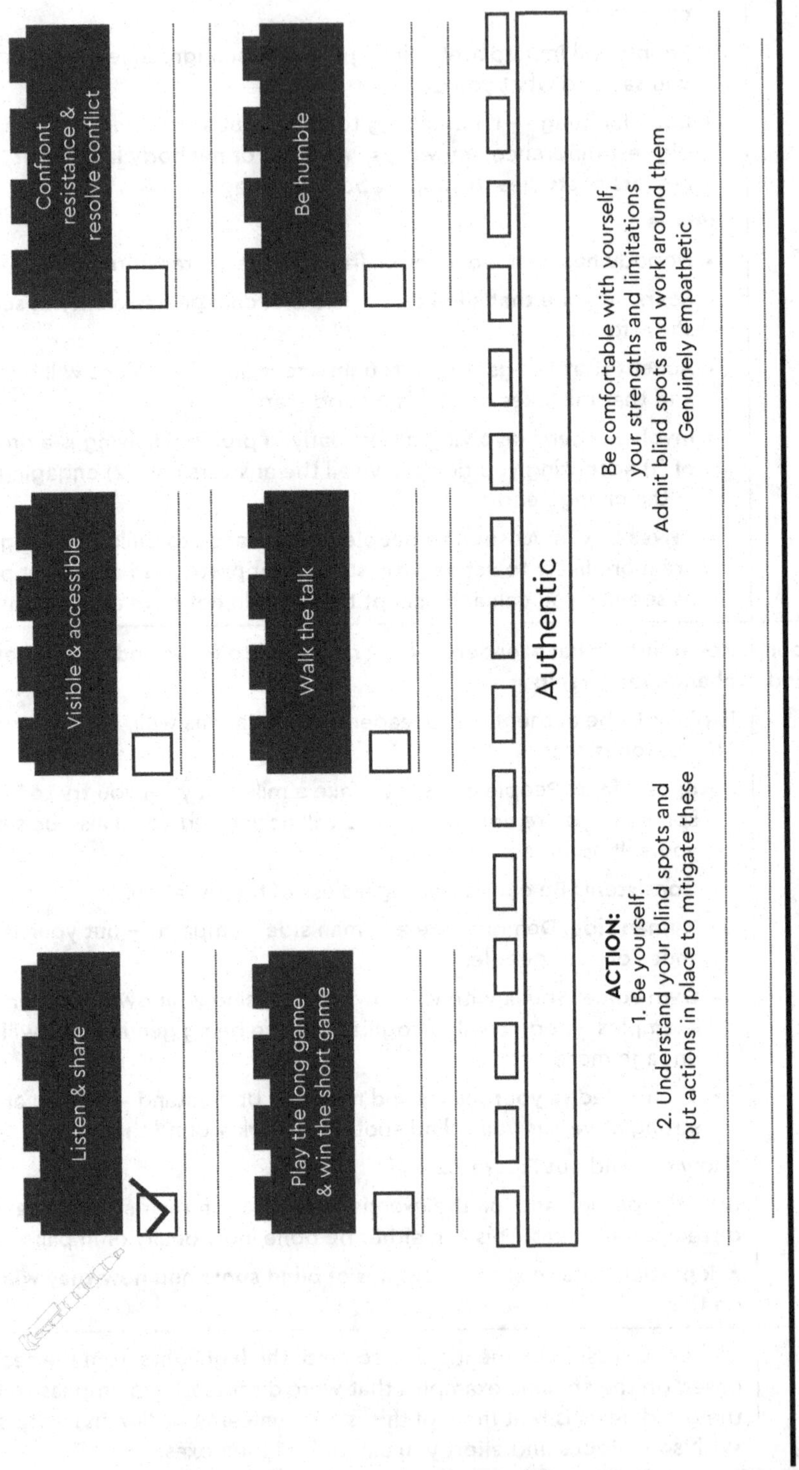

Listen & share
Visible & accessible
Confront resistance & resolve conflict
Play the long game & win the short game
Walk the talk
Be humble
Authentic
ACTION:
1. Be yourself.
2. Understand your blind spots and put actions in place to mitigate these
Be comfortable with yourself, your strengths and limitations
Admit blind spots and work around them
Genuinely empathetic

Figure 7.2 Exercise on good change leadership.

Change Learning Groups

What Is It?

Change initiatives are now rolling out and people are starting to adopt new processes and behaviors. It's important to keep an ear on the ground to listen and observe what is happening locally. What's important is finding a way to help share experiences, recognize where things may be falling down, and ensure everyone feels listened to and supported.

The Change Learning Group is a forum where everyone involved with, and affected by, the change comes together and shares their experiences. Peer support is very important at this time, but it's also essential that leaders are present to use the feedback to either reshape the narrative or even rethink a new approach. This is the time to bring the change catalysts[1] into play and let them take an active role. So it's a simple feedback approach that allows you to capture qualitative insights about what is or is not working for teams during the change journey. It also serves as an opportunity for peer learning as people exchange challenges and solutions.

This is the time when you should start planning the implementation of Change Learning Groups to fit within your Change Adoption Measures and be ready to go live with the Change Learning Groups as the changes are launched. The Change Learning Groups can run throughout the implementation of the change (from personalizing, navigating, and into living the change) so you can keep open a channel of insight and feedback back into the project from the teams.

Why It Matters?

There will always be challenges, issues, and bumps in the road on any change journey. These challenges create problems for people in their day-to-day work. Unless we can "debug" these issues quickly, people will get stuck and lose faith in the new ways of working. They will also feel like their problems are being ignored and will seek workarounds or ways to operate outside of the frame that has been set by the change.

If we can understand what's going wrong, then we can take action and remove the barriers preventing people from moving smoothly through their individual change journeys. It helps to keep them moving forward and builds belief that the change effort can succeed. Equally, where we see examples of good practice and success, we can share these with other teams and business areas.

Finally, the act of bringing people together to share and spar on their problems will provide a natural driver for the change journey – when people feel they are part of a shared experience, they move more quickly through their change curve.

How to Bring It into Action?

- Create a safe environment in which individuals feel able to share openly and honestly.
- Ensure the conversation stays productive by encouraging participants to help each other come up with three actions they can take to come unstuck

if they are finding it hard to adopt the new behaviors or to work within the new framework.

- It's not all about sharing what is going wrong – this is also a chance to celebrate success and share how we've been implementing, learning, and growing through the change.

If possible, try to embed Change Learning Groups into your Change Adoption Measures so you have a strong channel of qualitative feedback into the project that you can act on quickly. On a practical level, use the guide to help you plan the sessions and frame the content. You can be as flexible as you like with the groups in terms of how many, which teams, how often, etc. – it just depends on the nature of your project and how much capacity is available to mobilize sessions.

How to Set It Up?

Consider the following key questions in planning your Change Learning Groups. Remember, what works for one change project or business area might not work for another.

How Often?

What would work best? Weekly, bi-weekly, monthly, quarterly? Remember you might need a shorter cadence to start with but then stretch this out longer as you progress through the project lifecycle.

Who and How Many?

How many groups should run? How do you get good coverage of impacted teams? How many people in each group? From which level in the organization should people join? The dosing and mix will depend heavily on your project but, at a minimum, make sure key groups are covered and that you always speak to those that actually do the work.

Consolidate and Share?

How will you capture key inputs, themes, and feedback? Who will you share this output with? You can use the content guidance below to frame what you will capture. Consider sharing with the project team, steering committee, leaders, and even wider. You should also, if possible, integrate the Change Learning Group feedback into your Change Adoption Measures.

Act

When you have feedback, how are you going to respond? What actions will you take? You might review inputs with the project team and key leaders and then agree on solutions to take forward. Be sure to share best practices and solutions as well as problems.

How to Guide the Dialogues?

Simplicity is key and conversations will naturally provide rich insight. Consider starting with just three key questions and then adjusting as necessary. Also, adjust the duration of sessions depending on who is attending – but between 30 and 60 minutes should be enough.

1. What do you see working well within your teams right now?
2. What do you (see people) struggle with?
3. What are the key actions we could take that would make the biggest difference to your teams?

Be Creative...

Sometimes logistics don't work in our favor – getting face time with teams just isn't possible due to schedules and location. Consider some of the following options that could also act as a format for the same type of insight:

- **Virtual calls or face-to-face sessions:** Ensure that the relevant people can attend.
- **Yammer (Yam Jams):** Set up a Yammer community and encourage people to share their stories of success and how they overcome obstacles as and when they happen.
- **Feedback walls:** Create a wall where employees can publicly post feedback for everyone to see. This creates a strong signal around transparency and openness.
- **Suggestion boxes (e.g., virtual box):** Create a suggestion box and ask people to drop in any suggestions for change and improvements. Make sure that someone takes ownership of the box and feeds this back to the leaders, and in turn, that the results are shared with the larger community.
- **Change catalysts:** This is a great opportunity to call on your catalysts – they can help be a supporting voice in the room, a powerful presence in online communities, and a confidant for those more comfortable sharing in one-on-one meetings.

There are many different options and approaches to Change Learning Groups – most important is that peers are coming together to help each other to learn rather than teach each other. Individuals are invited to share their challenges or learnings when it comes to living the new processes and systems and using them in daily business. In this next example, a challenge/learning is shared from their own perspective and, through pertinent questions, discussion and sharing of experiences help see possible ways forward.

Inspirational Example of What a Change Learning Process Can Look Like

Step 1
Introduction of the challenge
	• One individual of the team introduces and briefly explains one of his/her challenges or learnings. It should be concise, while sharing some of following information:
	  • Sufficient context and background information.
	  • The help they need from the group.
	  • Their own view of the challenge.
	  • What they have already done and tried.
	  • What they are thinking of doing.

Step 2 Exploration of the challenge	• Group members explore the challenge by asking questions. They mainly use open questions and may explore deeper levels of intervention; how the challenge is approached, collaboration with others, and individual challenges.
Step 3 Definition of the challenge	• The Individual, having heard these, again formulates their question if needed.
Step 4 Consultation	• The group is discussing the topic brought forward. Does the group have similar learnings or challenges? • What actions should be taken? Can the action be solved by the challenge holder – or the group? Should the action be escalated?
Step 5 Actions and next steps	• The individual evaluates the consultation process: experiences, and the effects of group members' contributions. • What actions will be taken as a result of this discussion? And who will be responsible for the action?
Rotation	A new round can be started up with a new individual from the team.

CASE STUDY: CHANGE LEARNING GROUPS IN ELEMENT DESIGN

– Helle Liltorp Johnson, Project Manager, Element Design

One of the people from the LEGO Core teams mentioned that they had never tried implementations or changes that followed up the way we did it here, where you actually go back to the team and ask them about the impact on their end, and how it was working…

CONTEXT OF THE SPEED TO MARKET PROGRAM

The Speed to Market Context was already described in other cases.[2] In this case study, Helle is explaining her role in the project – and how she was supporting the organization by implementing the Change Learning Group approach as a way to follow up on the business benefits, new behaviors, and in general how the changes were working after go-live to engage, learn, and cross correct where needed.

> I was hired into the team as Project Manager when the project was already up and running. My role was to orchestrate activity, monitor progress, and cross correct if needed. My onboarding started by following up on the current status, creating oversight, and driving progress to move the needle on the different initiatives that had been implemented getting realization of the business benefits. A lot of work had been done already when I got on board, and it was really important to follow up and ensure that it was implemented well and that the changes were working as the team had imagined them to. The team was in a bit of turmoil due to changes as new people came on board and others were stepping out, so it was very dynamic and important to keep focus on the progress. The handovers were super important as the focus was on ways of working – and that required some effort to onboard new team members and provide them with the needed knowledge to continue progress on agreements for future collaborations as this project was about to change the way teams were working together across the organization.

We Started the Learning Processes through Pilot Initiatives

> We wanted to test and learn the new ways of working so we discussed different options on doing simulations, games, and role-plays before the actual implementation. But we ended up conducting two pilot initiatives to evaluate if we could succeed in getting the lead time reductions as planned. We chose two different projects as there were elements in those two projects that were applicable to testing lead time improvement on. So this was to try out the theory we had defined and whether it would work in practice before going live with the new ways of working. We had "workshopped" a lot in the Kaizen events on how to optimize the process, but we needed to test it out in real life to demonstrate that it could work.

The first pilot, we chose was with a very experienced Element Lead. There was a big potential here as there were many LEGO elements to be developed within a certain time frame, and this was also to test the lead time reduction on the elements where we depended on input and approval from an external partner. We had a strong person in this case who could drive this through and, at the same time, would allow us to leverage the elements that could help with lead time reductions. We took some things out of the equation, as we cannot always secure commitments from external partners, but here we were collaborating with a partner we knew well. So it was about creating optimal conditions.

For the other pilot, we deliberately chose a different situation with another external partner. We were curious to learn what would happen in a situation with more uncertainty and we wanted to test if we could absorb the uncertainties in our own set-up when working with an external partner. And, additionally, this case had LEGO elements that would also have to run in the front-end set-up – meaning elements that would require new and possibly never-seen-before solutions with great uncertainty if they would work. I visualized the timeline and in the follow-ups we marked where they were in the process, and how long they took in each of the subprocesses. Based on what we learned from the pilots and the input we received, we adjusted to get ready for the go-live.

The Change Learning Groups

We set up Change Learning Groups to follow the first teams, teams where we had an allocated Element Lead. It had to be in just such a process as we did not have sufficiently trained Element Leads to cover the full portfolio from the start. Some of the most well-founded teams were actually our core teams, and we selected those as we really needed speed from the beginning. So, in the end, it was six teams and that required a lot of effort in preparing, conducting, and following up on the sessions. But we invested in it and could definitely see the value. And timing was key – to do it right after go-live which was planned strategically to start when a new portfolio began.

I called in the core teams for the dialogues in the sessions along with the creative leads and the project leaders. I started each session by outlining the case for change and why we were doing it and then we got some very specific feedback on whether it was working as anticipated or if there were still uncertainties. We received a lot of constructive feedback which was documented: improvements, things that should be more clear, and also the things that worked well. We also communicated back to the project team, as they had worked hard on defining the new processes, and shared what things were working well and where we needed to create more synergies. In most cases, the Creative Leads and the Project Leads had ideas and suggestions on how to improve and what to do differently. So often the outcome of the sessions were some very specific suggested actions that I could bring back to the team.

The dialogues were informal with a structure based on the key changes that ensured we covered everything, and there would typically be areas with many inputs as well as areas without any feedback.

One of the guys from the core team mentioned that they had never tried implementations or changes that followed what we had done here, where you actually go back to the team and question to ask them on the impact from their end and how it was working. So just that part was very new for them in a LEGO context. When we actually reached out actively to get feedback, we knew that we were implementing something new and that this would change ways of working with the intent that it will improve – how do you experience something like this? I received this as very positive feedback – the way that this was expressed by the team. I asked them for 30 minutes of their time and one of our concerns was that those teams were super busy and it was going to be online due to COVID. We were really not sure that they would prioritize the sessions.

But I was super positively surprised that the Creative Leads and Project Leads prioritized those sessions, and if they could not join would send a representative from the team who talked about it with the rest of the team as preparation for our session. I set it up in a way that they had access to the file as a reminder of the changes we had implemented and the feedback they provided last time. I told them that the feedback would be shared back with the project team, so we could work with the feedback and corrective initiatives if needed. We started the session by following up on the input from the previous session to ensure that improvements happened based on their input. It was very well received – and all of the groups kept prioritizing the meetings, even though they ran over several months because they saw the need.

The sessions provided time for them to reflect on the change impacts and how it was working for them as a core team. So, for them, it was also to make a retrospective, reflect, and have a dialogue on what was working and what was not working. It was also a free and safe space for them to provide input and to be heard and listened to – because we asked them if the changes were working as anticipated.

We had previously agreed with the leadership team that we should not push the new processes on people if they did not work. Even though a lot of time was spent on designing the new processes, we also had to be brave enough to acknowledge if and when the new improvements were not working as expected. And that would force us to go back to the drawing board. It was also good for the team to reflect and get other views on it. So we were always ready to take the actions needed.

This was the most structured approach to change I have ever tried, getting feedback and then going back to work on it with the feedback. In some situations, we got the same feedback from different teams and we could see a pattern. When more teams were saying the same thing there was definitely an issue. When we found patterns, the input allowed us to work together on how to solve it and take the right actions to adjust.

We were running the sessions for 30 minutes and for a start it was every two weeks – after that, every month. A couple of times I got an email from one of the teams in the Change Learning Group, that they had experienced a challenge or something came up, and they knew who to reach out to if they had feedback.

In the Element Design initiative, there were many stakeholders at different levels and it was a big organization involved in this initiative. Helle explains how the outcomes and the learnings were communicated and shared:

It worked in a way that we consolidated data, as we had quite a lot of data based on the input we received. We decided not to provide downloads every week, but instead to consolidate and identify patterns, and based on that, we made a monthly download to the Speed to Market program team as a consolidated summary. It was both focused on the learnings and the actions or initiatives we were reacting to and these were reported up the chain directly into the Transformation Dashboard[3] on lead times, behaviors, learnings, and actions.

Leadership Involvement

We involved the Element Design leadership team to a great extent and that resulted in a lot of progress as well. When communicating to the leadership team, it allowed the leaders to provide successes and good feedback to their teams. One of the big challenges when we set out on the sessions was that some of the key players in the organization did not feel involved in the creative process, which made it difficult for them to understand the value they should create in the product. It felt as though they were just being asked to produce without any understanding. So one of the outcomes of all this that stood out for me as being very valuable was that we made an impact on motivation and satisfaction in those teams due to the changes we implemented. By making such a huge impact on the core teams, suddenly there was a strong passion to create toys again, and this was a great win. We were sitting on something we considered the jewel of our business which is the LEGO brick – and if we don't think it is fun and engaging to produce, why should our consumers consider it fun to play with?

We celebrated that we reduced the number of emails and meetings – and increased the level of engagement and synergies of involvement of key players in the process. This was a big win both in relation to lead time reduction and increased motivation. One of our leaders called the increased motivation the "Shining Eyes" – and we got a lot of feedback on many more "Shining Eyes" in the organization and how, in general, the atmosphere in the teams improved.

At the same time, there was a certain level of humbleness in the leadership team knowing what it takes to change ways of working. I was in doubt if the leaders as well would show up to the reporting sessions, but they did. The leaders were also aware that there was a lot of motivation and satisfaction at stake here. And they realized that instead of pushing it out to a project team to work on this, they would have bigger success in their teams by engaging themselves and working together with the project team.

The key changes formed the framework – and that was recognizable to everyone. And it was driven in a very structured way combined with an easy way of understanding the current status and progress. Everyone understood what we were talking about. And the core teams were brilliant in explaining this with specific examples. So when those examples were brought up, everyone knew which elements we were talking about and which situations around the elements had been either challenging or successful. Everybody could relate to it. And that made it powerful.

The combination of calling out the successes and the structured way of following up on the impact and results of key changes made a big difference. And, additionally, it brought the teams much closer together based on the open dialogues and the high level of engagement.

TOP TIP

- When navigating change, great change leadership should be brought into play.
- Ensure you take action rather than just gather feedback. And share what actions you've taken with the Change Learning Groups so they can see you are responding to their concerns.
- Although leaders may not participate directly in Change Learning Groups, they should remain close to group outputs to be able to monitor progress and action feedback.

SIGNS YOU'RE READY TO MOVE FORWARD...

- The majority of measures and subjective opinions suggests the change is becoming normal working practice.
- Success stories are emerging and circulating.
- Leaders feel less need for support from the change team.

Notes

1. See Chapter 5 to understand more about change catalysts.
2. See Chapters 3 and 4.
3. See Chapter 7 to understand more about the Transformation Dashboard.

CHAPTER 8

MOMENT 5 – LIVING THE CHANGE

What Is It?

Once the process of driving change has subsided, the new ways of working may have taken hold and people should be committing to them – it's now becoming part of normal operations. This is where people can reconnect with the purpose for the change and review what they've achieved.

Possible signs that suggest we need help living the change

People are sliding back into old habits or saying that things will "get back to normal" soon.

- If you ask people about the change, they consider it finished
- People don't remember why they've been through the changes
- KPIs/metrics are not being met

How people are feeling

- "I'm relieved – it was difficult at times, but we got there"
- "I'm glad we did this – I can really see the difference it's making"
- "I'm restless – when can we change the next thing?"
- "I'm glad it's over – we've finished changing now"
- "I'm nostalgic – I miss the old ways"
- "I'm tired"

DOI: 10.4324/9781003243113-8

Why It Matters?

If we get this moment right, we'll get:

- Business benefits realized
- New high-fliers, networks, and communities
- Long-lasting capability
- Positive reputation for change

If we don't get it right:

- Old ways start to make a stealthy return
- A false end point
- Demoralized workforce and "change scars"
- Fatigue

How and Where Can You Have the Biggest Impact?

Where	How
Frame a sense of progress, e.g., Transformation Dashboard, to ensure that you realize the business benefits and the new behaviors are well anchored in the organization.	**Transformation Dashboard page 157**
When it comes to keeping the change alive, we can't ignore the social and cultural context in which people are trying to put their new ways of working into action and making the change "stick."	**Keeping It Alive page 175**

Transformation Dashboard – Measuring and Anchoring Change

What Is It?

A Transformation Dashboard is a way to create visibility to whether projects, changes, and transformations are delivering as expected and to the committed benefits. This will show us if the organization has committed to and delivered the change activities. More importantly, we also need to test whether or not the change is being adopted by the target audience.

- Are they adopting new ways of working?
- Are they sticking to the new process?
- Are they using the new system?
- Are they demonstrating the required behaviors?

■ Are we seeing early signs of the business benefit identified in the business case for the project?

Remaining close to the change experience seems obvious, but many organizations get this wrong. They are over-reliant on reports and opinions from leaders. To get a more accurate picture of whether changes are being adopted, we need to go deeper and understand what is really happening. By doing this, we can quickly identify if we are going off-track and agree on corrective actions or, if things are going well, identify and share success stories.

This approach offers a structured way to follow up on changes and assigns key measures to track the progress of the change while providing the mechanics of how you will get this information and monitor it over time with both behavioral and business impact measures. The more traditional way would be to measure progress based on business impact measures, for example, financial measures, cost reduction, or reduction in workload or lead times. The more holistic approach includes behavioral indicators and individual change journeys which are included to ensure that the new behaviors are sticking. It's valuable to define transformation metrics before change implementation or before we kick off new ways of working as this creates clarity on what success looks like.

Why It Matters?

Many change efforts fail for various reasons – several related to lack of anchoring the transformation. One reason could be that "victory" is declared too soon. After a period of hard work, it can be tempting to declare victory with the first clear performance improvement. Behavioral changes need time and effort to sink deeply into the culture, and new approaches are fragile and subject to regression. Additionally, it can be the fact that the change is not anchored in and owned by the culture.

Until the new behaviors are rooted in the norms and shared values and become "the way we do things around here," they are subject to degradation as soon as the pressure for change is removed.

How to Bring It into Action?

Use the steps outlined in the tool to define your adoption measures and how you will measure them. You should then use the Transformation Dashboard to track progress through the change. You will also need to decide at what point and level you will follow up and whether you will have one Dashboard for the whole project or if you need separate dashboards for different audience groups. Also, for example, if you will follow up at a global or local level.

Realistically you will start planning your transformation metrics/adoption measures right from the start of the project. However, you might not be able to finalize your measures and how you will track them until just before you launch your change initiatives toward the end of Moment 2 (Understanding the Change).

You will start tracking the adoption measures in Moment 4 (Navigating the Change) once teams have started to engage with and test out the new ways of working. Ideally, you will continue to track them until you transition to sustainability planning as part of the handover to the business when the project scales down and officially closes. In this overview, you find a guide on how to set up a Transformation Dashboard (Figure 8.1). Each of the four steps is described in the next section.

Step 1: Identify Adoption Measures – Additional Guidance and Examples (Figure 8.2)

All change projects vary, so the adoption measures will too. Some examples are given below to help with your thinking, but at a minimum, try to use the four key components as a frame of reference for your measures. In addition, you need to make sure that there is a way to get either qualitative or quantitative data on your measures, otherwise it's impossible to track them!

Step 2: Agree on Tracking Method – Additional Guidance and Examples (Figure 8.3)

There are many different ways to harvest qualitative and quantitative data relating to adoption measures. Some inspiration is given below on the methods you can use and also how to create the red/yellow/green benchmark ratings. Remember – change is not an exact science so don't worry too much about perfecting these. You can always adjust in real time as you learn!

Step 3: Track Adoption Measures – Additional Guidance and Examples (Figure 8.4)

The Dashboard below can be used to capture and track your measures. You will need to adjust the columns on the right to reflect your cadence (e.g., monthly, weekly, daily) and can even transfer quantitative data into graph format for visual factories.

Step 4: Relapse Prevention and Course Correction (Figure 8.5)

Once the measures are live and you are tracking progress, you will need to respond in real-time to issues so you can drive measures toward green rather than see them deteriorate to red. Here is a simple guide that you could consider implementing to ensure the feedback and action loop is complete. Try to use the Change Learning Groups[1] approach as part of your insight gathering for the adoption measures. This will provide a qualitative level of input around what specifically is or is not working. You could track this as part of a "Relapse Prevention" measure (e.g., key issues from feedback resolved) and use the insights as a key driver for corrective actions in the above model.

1. IDENTIFY ADOPTION MEASURES	2. AGREE TRACKING METHOD	3. TRACK ADOPTION MEASURES	4. RELAPSE PREVENTION
Firstly, define the key adoption measures that you are going to track through the change. To do this it is best to work through ideas with the project team and business leads on the project rather than on your own (e.g., in a short workshop or brainstorming call).	After you have agreed your adoption measures, you need to work out how you will track them. Methods will vary significantly here depending on what is readily available through existing business data vs. where you need to go and seek new information.	Before you kick-off, you need to answer two key questions: **1. How frequently are we going to refresh the dashboard?** This will vary significantly by project and may also change within the lifecycle of your project. For example, it often makes sense to have a short cadence to begin with then a longer cadence once things are more stable. As a minimum, you should aim for a monthly update but ideally aim for bi-weekly in the early stages of a change being launched.	The whole point of the adoption measures is to tell you whether or not your change is working and to make the change stick. If your adoption measures start showing yellow or red then you need to take action rather than just watch. Equally, if you are seeing green in some business areas for a single measure, but red elsewhere, you can transfer good practice.
The measures will vary depending on the change you are delivering and also how easy they are to define and track. In all cases, the question you are trying to answer is:	Also, your measures will be a combination of quantitative data (e.g., sales KPIs) and qualitative data (e.g., verbal reports of behavioural adoption).		You need to decide how you will react to issues and opportunities flagged
'What indicators will tell us that teams are adopting this change rather than rejecting it?'	After you have agreed your tracking method, you will then need to assign benchmarks to each adoption measure so you can state whether they are:	**2. With whom will we share it & when?** The measures will be useful insight for a range of stakeholders. You need to agree who will get access and when. This will vary by project but a recommendation would be to review within the project team first, then share with your steering committee and key stakeholders.	The simplest way to do this is, when you review the measures with the project team and business leads, agree: 1. What action needs to be taken immediately? 2. What are the 'watch outs' that we will act upon if we see them appear next time? 3. Where do we have opportunities to share learnings?
As a frame you should always consider the following 3 key components: 1. **Individual Change Journey** 2. **Behavioural Indicators** 3. **Business Metrics**	1. On-track (green) 2. Below target (yellow) 3. A problem (red)		
You will find further guidance on how to define trackable measure in the next chapter	With all of this in place, you have your adoption measures dashboard almost ready to go.		

Figure 8.1 Setting up the transformation dashboard.

Component	Description	Examples
Individual Change Journey	Measures that give an indication of whether sufficient progress is being made in the psychological change journey of individuals. Have people fundamentally bought into and committed to the change?	• Rationale (the 'why') is fully understood • Individual commitment to the change • Attitude towards the change • Willingness to persist with the changes • Understanding of what needs to change in their role/day-to-day work
Behavioural Indicators	Indicators that people are shifting their behaviours and adopting new ways of working. Visible signs that something is changing. It's important to test these at both a leadership and non-leadership level. Behavioural indicators should be as specific as possible – something you can answer yes or no to when you measure.	• Number of logins to new tool/platform • % of orders going through new online system • New 'language' being used within teams • Individuals adapting their work and relationships to the changes • Leaders reinforcing new ways of working
Business Metrics	Operational, commercial, or business metrics that show us whether or not the changes delivered are having the intended impact on overall business performance.	• Sales figures • Leadtimes • Error rates • Customer satisfaction scores/net promoter score • Pulse scores/employee satisfaction
Relapse Prevention	Measures which tell us whether or not people are going back to or reinforced for old ways of working. Whether people are abandoning the change effort.	• Logins/use of old system • Evidence of old process use • Use of old 'language' • Evidence of leaders not role modelling the change/reinforcing the change • Resolution of issues raised by team

Figure 8.2 Identify adoption measures.

Tracking Methods

- Business metrics from Ops systems
- Customer data
- Pulse data
- E2E process times
- System login data
- System usage data
- Surveys – rating scales
- Surveys – qualitative comments
- Interviews
- Change Learning Group discussions
- Change agent dialogues
- Polling apps
- Feedback wall
- 360
- 'Field' research/observation

Benchmarking

When you have agreed on your adoption measures and how you will track them, you need to define some simple benchmarks which will allow you to rate measures. Guidance is provided below, but it's important to remember that with many changes, especially those that are more behavioural in nature, you might see a slow burn in before the change sticks – so yellow rather than green in the early stages after launch.

1. On-track (green):
What we would hope and expect to see if the majority (not all) of the target audience are deliberately committing to and engaging with the changes.

1. Below target (yellow)
What we would expect to see if there is traction but not widespread engagement with the change. In this circumstance things could go either way (i.e. green or red) quickly unless support is provided or change efforts are sustained.

1. A problem (red)
What we would expect to see if the majority of the target audience are not committing to or engaging with the change. The sort of result that would make you immediately seek urgent action

Example Measure Benchmarks	On Track	Below Target	A Problem
Commitment to make the change work (survey question, 100% = full)	>75%	25-75%	<25%
Average logins per person per day to new online sales tool (expect 2/day)	>1.5	0.5-1.5	<0.5

Figure 8.3   Agree on tracking method.

Component	Adoption Measure	Tracking Method	Benchmarks	m1	m2	m3	m4	m.
Individual Change Journey	Commitment to make the change work	Monthly survey (100% = full)	On Target = >75%, Below Target = 25-75%, A problem = <25%	60	65	50	30	20
Behavioural Indicators								
Business Metrics								
Relapse Prevention								

Figure 8.4 Track adoption measures.

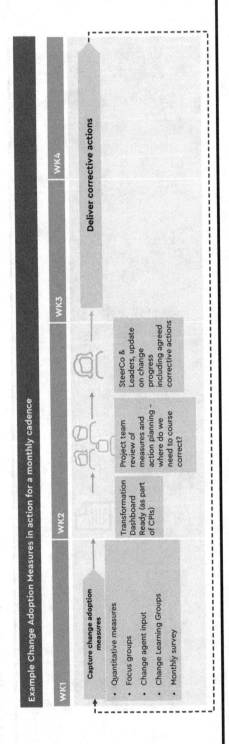

Figure 8.5 Preventing relapse & course correct.

CASE STUDY: USING A TRANSFORMATION DASHBOARD TO STEER PROGRESS AND ENSURE ANCHORING

Along with the celebrations and balloons in the go-live events went the change agents, and shortly after that we were back to where we started.

– Jan Juul Severinsen, Head of Portfolio Management and Palle Ditlevsen, Sr. Business Manager

CONTEXT OF THE SPEED TO MARKET PROGRAM

In this case study, you will understand how the Speed to Market Transformation was anchored through the use of the Transformation Dashboard and the transformation metrics just described. Severinsen was the owner of the LEGO Development Process and, at the same time, he was part of the Steering Committee of the program and owner of the transformation. Ditlevsen[2] was the Business Lead and the overall architect overseeing the program objectives. They are here briefly sharing the context of Speed to Market from a portfolio perspective.

> The rapidly changing world required us to rethink the timing of critical portfolio decisions. This was what triggered Speed to Market to get started. Our commercial ambition was to make a portfolio that resonated the best way possible with consumers in the market. This required us to push selected portfolio decisions as late as possible and we decided to create a process speed capability allowing us to execute launch projects within the shorter timeline. But then there were a lot of underlying advantages to making early decisions such as from the aspect of level loading – for example, how we plan and level the production workload that is needed to bring the portfolio to market. If we make all the decisions at the same time, you create peaks in the workload, but that is more of an internal optimization opportunity.
>
> We had very strong top management commitment, from our CEO, COO, and CPMO, and they requested regular updates, which we were delivering according to our agreements. This ensured that we had our hands on the "hot plate" and took the risks needed with a high level of personal engagement. We did not just step away when things got tough, and it was tough many times. We had a lot of commitment, but we were lacking in funds (out-of-pocket costs) allocated. And that was a challenge as we did not have the opportunity to go out and find the IT solutions, or have a new solution made. All of these things impacted the motivation of the team. It was difficult for them to understand the importance of the initiative, but we actually succeeded with a strong focus on optimizing ways of working through use of internal resources.
>
> In relation to the work with external business partners, there was big potential and a need for reducing lead times. The team took external,

e.g., movie franchises, into their assessment working together with these companies. The LEGO Group had seen a reduced and declining production timeline within the movie industry forcing the company to get reference materials later in the process.

If we were able to make a portfolio that was more relevant and desirable and that hopefully translated into higher accuracy, then consumer sales would yield bigger commercial value. What does value look like for the organization? The whole leveling of workload should result in a better work–life balance where we can avoid those very busy peaks – hopefully, this would enable individuals to be better in flow with their tasks.

This also drove a sense of belonging through the initiatives we worked across functions. It created the feeling and understanding of being part of a bigger chain. It also created better working relations on the end-to-end path. We came from a situation where the process was standardized but then we optimized more narrowly in the smaller teams. Based on those shifts we needed to find each other in new ways and more holistically, and we were allowed to revisit our go-to-market and a new product development process which also brought more motivation. People received my work on the other end, and it actually made a big difference whether I did a good job or not, and I could understand why I had to do the things I did.

An important element when we were reviewing was how to work faster without creating more workload. One of the findings was how we could improve first-time-through without creating loops in the process, where things began circling. Being more aware of what actually determines a good quality output helped people to bring good quality to the next step in the process.

Just like any other manufacturing company, we are organized into functional areas. And we have people working on development projects who did not talk to each other because they followed the same routines and always knew what was happening. Then, suddenly, all these dynamics came into play and we actually needed to reinvent how we interacted with each other. Solving problems among different functional areas was an eye-opener on what a big impact you can actually have by changing the process.

We were able to reduce the LEGO Development Process significantly. The goal was to make it more digestible. We did not push for lead time reduction where we knew it could not be done. We said that it's a subset to make the task more digestible for the overall organization. Nevertheless, what we saw was that in some steps of the processes, the solutions that were identified for the majority of the portfolio could be applied to the rest as well. So there were a lot of positive spillover effects that could be harvested. That was another positive outcome of some of the work in the project streams.

Anchoring the Transformation

In order to anchor the transformation, the first thing we did was to have a change partner allocated to the program. We knew that the program was impacting the organization and that the vast majority of the changes were behavioral changes. You need to apply the skills of a change practitioner or a transformation expert – we cannot take for granted that everybody and all leaders are familiar with this and everybody thinks first about change. The organization needed to be reminded and guided, and I think that is done best by having people dedicated to serve that perspective and having them co-located into the environment that is changing.

It's important to understand that this was a phased process and we did not take on all the project streams at one time. We said, "Let's tackle this first," and then take the next one. Otherwise, we could not really see our way through it. And one of the dawning realizations we got was that after the implementation of the first stream of development process improvements, we actually had a lot of strong support for the change management part. But after this initial implementation, the program leaders, transformation consultants, and change agents had to refocus their attention on the next stream to start working on their improvements. Approximately 3 months after the first implementation, it became worrisome for some of us ... did we really succeed in anchoring the initial improvements or had we kind of left the organization without knowing how to follow up? Were we getting the improvements and benefits that we were expecting instead of just focusing on where we are now?

This was where Severinsen, as the ultimate owner of the transformation, got a little bit concerned. He wondered if they were slipping back from the first initiatives and if they would be sustainable. That is where he agreed to revisit all the improvements made previously which was the backdrop for why he saw the need to make a holistic view of the change and not just look at the implementation.

This was a way to remobilize leaders and have the steering team support the investment required to establish a more well-functioning transformation by making a dedicated transformation team that could figure out how to organize and track the transformation. And within that team, one of the things we did really well was to seek input and feedback from the business drivers on the individual projects in addition to bringing in the book of theory. They also requested to be kept accountable and they wanted to see that the other streams were held accountable as well. So there was some pull and interest to see how the bigger picture of the program was functioning and succeeding. And we actually managed to convince all the business leaders leaning into this Transformation

Dashboard that it could do this fairly simply with some valuable metrics that would be understood by a very broad team of functional experts.

We realized that there were very different and subjective views of what was working and what was not based on the first implementation. There was a need to create an objective voice to set up a more objective view of the situation – and we had definitely celebrated the victory too soon. That was when we realized that something more long-term needed to be done. Along with the celebrations and balloons at the go-live events where the change agents went, we found ourselves back to where we started.

What we needed was to convert those subjective feelings into more data-driven measures. And we needed to know whether we succeeded in changing our behaviors to the extent that we were able to measure the business impact of the changes by measuring, for example, the lead times we were delivering against. What the Transformation Dashboard does across the whole chain is to make it extremely visible both for the individual sub-stream owners, as well as the entire group and our sponsors. Are we getting the impact on all dimensions that we are looking for?

This was a really, really strong result of working with the Transformation Dashboard. It was another way of seeing the impact of our ultimate aim of making decisions later in the process. Are we seeing this come to life? For me, this was an even bigger indicator that we were succeeding with the journey we set out to make and that we can actually make decisions on the accelerated part of the portfolio much later than we did previously. It was a living example of how we could make the acceleration of the development timelines come to life in the business as a result of the Transformation Dashboard, and we could see the impact on the business.

The big difference here was making the changes objective, visible, and sustainable. I don't know how many times we tried to implement changes previously and they did not stick because we were too busy doing other stuff and moving on to new initiatives. Most organizations work like that, where you are more motivated to move on to the next thing instead of making sure that what you have implemented is actually working and sticking. So it is important to make sure that someone has the obligation and responsibility to sustain the change and make sure that the identified benefits are realized.

In this context, we work in a development cycle, and when you try to change behaviors, that takes a long time to anchor. It becomes a long journey, but that is what it takes to change behaviors. Just looking back at the first changes we did in model design – that implementation was done almost three years ago – and we are still following up on it. We still use the training videos to understand why we are doing this when we bring in new people. We still have relevant discussions on this part of the process. This is just an indication of how difficult it can be to have changes like this fully engrained.

Why Do We Need Both Business Metrics and Behavioral Indicators?

It is easy to fall back into old routines and old ways of working because we have been working like this for many years. Having both business metrics and behavioral indicators provides a balance when you are trying to find a new solution to a problem. People tend to ask if it is really solving the problem. And, if yes, then everybody is happy, and we can see this in the metrics. But if we are not solving the problem and the problem remains, it is healthy to look into the behavioral indicators to see if we have changed what we agreed to change from a behavioral perspective. If we have done that, then is it actually the solution we created that is not working? You can have a situation where everybody is doing what they are supposed to, but it is not working. Then you need to go back to the drawing board and find another solution and other types of behaviors. You can also get into a situation where you are solving the problem, but people are not following the new ways of working, and this is when you need to find another smarter approach you can apply. But we have experienced that these go hand-in-hand, that where we are following the desired behaviors, we are also getting the expected impact.

Based on years of experience we have not yet been forced to change our ways of working – a little bit of headwind and a burning platform triggered us to change our ways of working, and we learned so much in doing so. The next time we have to make a significant shift we will have a better setup to do it.

Here is an example of visualization of the Speed to Market Transformation Dashboard.[3]

You find an example of a Transformation Dashboard (consisting of five streams/projects) in Figure 8.6 on page 170.

For each substream:

- Change Overview and Status – Figure 8.7
- Change Indicators (behavioral indicators) – Figure 8.8
- Transformation Plan – Figure 8.9
- Successes, Learnings & Actions – Figure 8.10

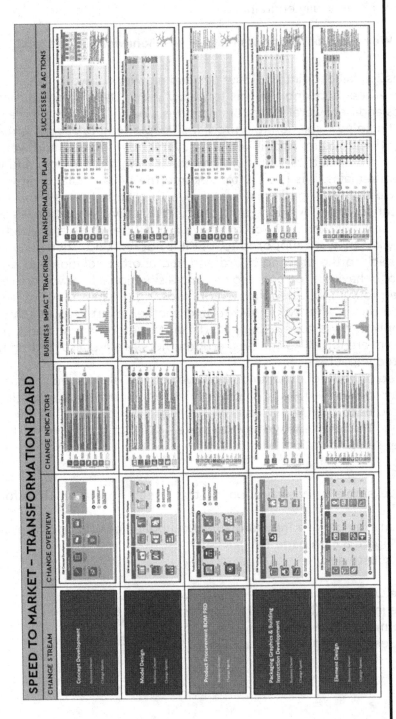

Figure 8.6 Overview of the Transformation Dashboard (example).

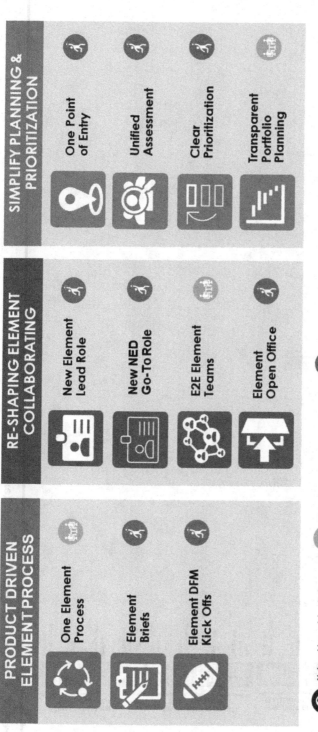

Figure 8.7   Change overview and status (example).

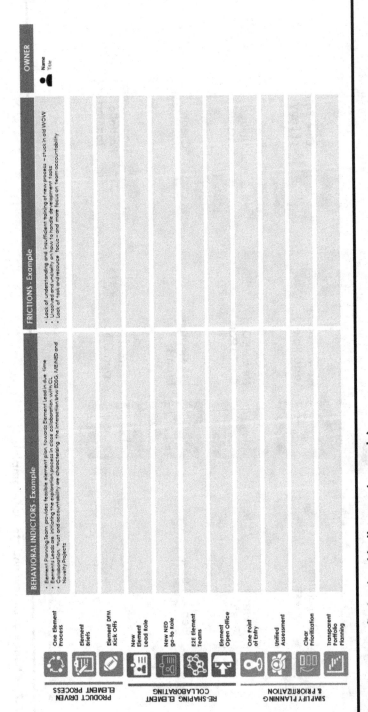

Figure 8.8 Change/behavioral indicators (example).

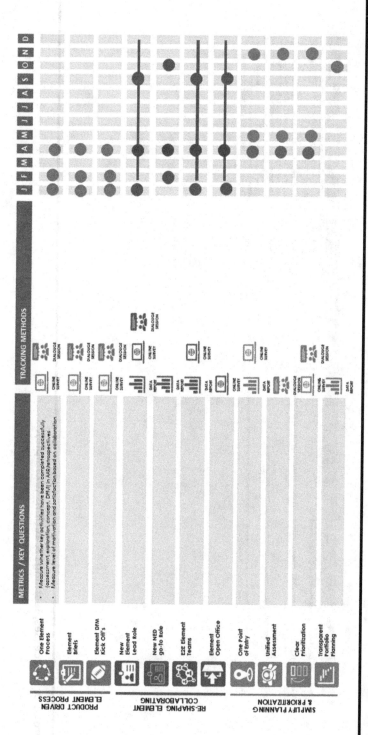

Figure 8.9   Transformation plan (example).

STREAM	ACTIONS	RESP.	DEADLINE
FMC Tool	New FMC Tool. Implemented by Q1 – Test in April	xxx	w24
One proces and E2E Teams	High Complex Elements – R&R, business ownership and process stream. (Status with Elizabeth w50, pilot with CPL in STM framework)	xxx	w23
STM survey 2	Next steps after the interviews – consolidate the input from the survey in April	xxx	w19
NED GO TO	Deep dive on IP Approval – how to ensure best collaboration/process and avoid misalignment in perceptions – meeting with EL + Guest Speaker IP approval	xxx	w20

LEARNINGS AND SUCCESSES

- NEO 2022 prefilled out and sendt to all projects has given visual timings overviews on a earlier stage to be shared across TLG.
- FCFC. Project would like to develop a flame and ring element. Original scope was 2k CMI solution. Through different cost scenario analysis, already in exploration, it become clear for the project to go for 2 x 1k solution instead. By that, we will have a more generic element and to a lower price. NED-go-to used knowledge from previous developed element for Ninjago (Dragon Coin). Benefit: Early maturity of element reducing leadtime.

Figure 8.10 Successes, learnings & actions (example).

Keeping It Alive

What Is It?

Ultimately, the LEGO Way of Change is an approach in which everyone embraces change as a part of their everyday routine and is eager and willing to see it as an opportunity not just for the business, but for them individually. Living the Change in turn means fully adopting this way of thinking and relating it specifically to the transformation they will have gone through, and continue to go through in most cases. When it comes to keeping the change alive, we can't ignore the social and cultural context. So what is the social and cultural context?

Social Context

No person is an island – putting change and learning into action involves engaging and involving people from all levels. Whether they're managers driving the change, peers, and catalysts supporting each other to sustain it, or leaders ensuring we stay aligned with a broader strategy and helping to communicate the vision, everyone has a part to play.

Cultural Context

The cultural characteristics of an organization can also facilitate or inhibit the adoption of change and knowledge transfer. In the world of psychology, this is called the "transfer climate"[4] and it includes things like our cultural attitude toward learning, systems and policies, and the shared practices we have that are related to learning. In the LEGO Group, there is already a strong history of supporting learning initiatives, so it's about harnessing that and creating a culture in which we believe that learning is essential to us and the work that we do.

Why It Matters?

To make learning stick, learning leaders need a fundamental shift in the way they think about change and learning – and where they focus on interventions to solve problems in the real world. When it comes to keeping the change alive, we can't ignore the social and cultural context in which people are trying to put their new ways of working into action and making the change "stick." Change is learning a new way of doing things and if we're not open to it or don't give ourselves the time to engage with it, we won't get very far.

How to Bring It into Action?

Social Context – What Can We Do?

For Managers and Leaders

Managers maximize opportunities as spotters and coaches. They should be on the ground finding new ways to keep the change alive and coaching individuals through it. They need to feel autonomous enough and empowered to make tweaks and changes if they spot something not working. They provide leaders with coaching support and set up regular conversations with them in which they can present ideas and provide solutions.

The last thing you want is for people to feel that the change was just another fad or leader-led initiative. Avoid "seagull management"[5] from leaders by helping them see how they can regularly participate in the conversation and stay visible. They provide an invaluable link between the work being done on the ground and the broader business vision and impact – use this to encourage them to regularly reshape and revisit their narrative and keep teams inspired. Seagull management is a leadership style where a manager or leader will only interact with employees when they think there is a problem, or when they feel like it. They come in, make hasty decisions about things they may have little understanding of as they're not on the ground, and leave a big mess after them which others have to deal with (in other words, swoop in, flap around, make a lot of noise and fly off again, leaving feathers and scattered papers in their wake).

Leaders and managers are having a critical role in being "role models" – this is a significant factor when we look at sustained behavior change. So it is an important matter to lead by example and walk the talk to drive the organizational change.[6]

For Peers

Use the change catalysts on the ground. Peer support has a direct impact on people putting their new behaviors and learning into action. The more people are engaged in the change, the more likely the desired behaviors will reach a tipping point and become the norm.

Cultural Context – What Can We Do?

Day-to-day pressures will threaten to overwhelm and keep us from putting the extra effort into trying new things or continuing to work at something which doesn't feel quite natural yet. At these times, it's important to keep our ears to the ground and consider what level of support is needed and whether we need to reinforce certain behaviors or reconnect to a central vision.

Reinforce

Set up discussion groups like Change Learning Groups[7] with leaders and managers that will allow you to celebrate success/achievements to date. Imagine reaching the point when the change is just part of normal working life. What will this look like? How will we know when we've made it to this point? How far away are we and what is needed to get there? For example, perhaps specific technical training is needed in a certain area and a higher level of engagement through Change Learning Groups.

Reconnect

■ Revisit your culture maps and re-evaluate your culture blockers and enablers. Use these to assess what you may need to do to develop or revise current and desired outcomes moving forward. Change is fluid and goalposts may change, so make sure your messaging and story keep up.

- Connect back to your vision[8] statement: Is it being lived? Has it changed? Are we still as clear on it now as we were at the start?
- Reconnect with your tools: Specifically, consider your Transformation Dashboard tool to monitor progress and the personal change maps which are part of the Make-It-Mine tool.[9] How might someone's change may be different now that they are seeing the change in practice? What are the benefits of this agility and flexibility?

Depending on what your journey has been like and/or where your priorities are, we use the below resources to help keep the conversation alive, reconnect and reinforce key behaviors, and create a culture of change:

1. Sharing change experience
2. Recognition/celebrate success – progress principle
3. Case study/journey videos
4. Personal contracts (story and figures)
5. Coaching/per feedback leaders
6. Booster sessions
7. Catalyst form/feedback
8. Pulse surveys, e.g., quarterly for the first year

Moment 5 is no longer critical if...

- People are forgetting the old way of working or the workforce no longer has a shared memory of how things were.
- Change is delivering KPIs over a sustained period.
- Leaders and stakeholders are aware that change is constant and not "done."

Notes

1. See Chapter 7 to understand more about Change Learning Groups.
2. Ditlevsen shared his leader story on how the Speed to Market Change Vision was created in Chapter 4.
3. No further quantified data is shown here as this is considered sensitive data.
4. Blume, B. D., Ford, J. K., Baldwin, T. T., Huang, J. L. (2010). Transfer of Training: A Meta-Analytic Review. Journal of Management. https://www.bing.com/ck/a?!&&p=f57b 7ec2afb919e8JmltdHM9MTY1OTUyNDE1MyZpZ3VpZD1mMTViMjBmZi1kNGI5LTRmY zgtOWRiMS05MGFkZDY3MWQyNjQmaW5zaWQ9NTE2OA&ptn=3&hsh=3&fclid= d801e36b-131a-11ed-9360-700bbdde8521&u=a1aHR0cHM6Ly9qb3VybmFscy5zYWdllc HViLmNvbS9kb2kvYWJzLzEwLjExNzcvMDE0OTIwNjMwOTM1Mjg4MA&ntb=1
5. Blanchard, Ken, PhD: One Minute Manager, 2015.
6. See Chapter 7 on What Great Change Leadership looks like to make the change sustainable.
7. See Chapter 7 for more inspiration on Change Learning Groups.
8. See Chapter 4 for more inspiration on Change Vision.
9. See Chapter 6 for more inspiration on Make-It-Mine tools.

CHAPTER 9

CONCLUSION AND VISIONARY VIEW OF THE FUTURE

Post-pandemic, and in the world in general, unpredictable changes and the need for transformation have become predictable. Reality requires us to quickly change the way we do things, often without a lot of time to prepare, plan, and execute. Any time a business or team experiences change, it takes time for people to get used to and internalize new behaviors or expectations. There is a need for leaders to prepare for rapid innovation and modifications in order to meet future needs based on new strategic directions, new patterns, and new trends. So, overall, there is a need for transforming today and tomorrow. So how can you create the future, while at the same time delivering today? It has become a critical leadership skill of finding the balance between today and tomorrow.

I see two dimensions surfacing when looking toward future needs in a transformational context – one is digital transformations and another is more in-depth understanding and focus on behavioral science to leverage understanding the people side of change, which will always be the constant element that makes a difference.

Digital Transformations

New technologies and constantly changing customer expectations mean processes and technologies might look completely different, even when thinking just a year ahead. And this requires organizations to be prepared and adopt change as a regular part of the company culture. To be able to meet and keep pace in these fast-changing environments, new terms such as "test & learn," "fail quickly," "flexibility," and "agile" are now becoming a natural part of the company culture.

DOI: 10.4324/9781003243113-9

By prioritizing agile transformations instead of, for example, waterfall approaches, the organization will need to be more willing to embrace adjustments as they come at a faster pace in this more forward-thinking work environment with more focus on new ways of working and always bringing new ideas or thoughts to the table. Here, the change interventions described in this book become even more important in order to lower resistance to change, thereby helping the organization to adjust in a more agile way. You could critically challenge if the LEGO Way of Change is fully adaptable and ready to be embedded into a fully agile context with a higher pace and faster iterations. No doubt that leveraging tools and interventions to be more founded toward on-demand learning strategies allowing leaders and practitioners to educate themselves at their own pace and when convenient for them would match better into a more agile environment. Still, some fundamental change leadership skills would be required to go into this direction.

Behavioral Science

Another approach that is rapidly gaining traction in organizations around the world is behavioral design, which based on behavioral science. Behavioral science is a combination of psychology, economics, and neuroscience. The use of these elements enables understanding, predicting, and influencing human behavior. As transformations become more complex, it is vital to better understand human behaviors and apply this understanding to improving transformational interventions. The level of success in changing human behaviors will always be what makes the biggest difference.

Behavioral science is all about studies on when and why individuals engage in specific behaviors by experimentally examining the impact of factors such as intentions, motivation, abilities, triggers, social influences, contextual effects, and habits. By deploying a behavioral design approach to transformations, more analysis work and data can be applied to understand the existing and new behaviors required so that more deliberate interventions are achieved. This helps organizations build more effective solutions and changes with lower rates of failure. By developing a deeper understanding of the problems to be solved, less time is spent on concepts and interventions that have no impact and more time on success with engaging the organization and individuals to an extent where the change is done with them and not to them. In this book, you have seen glimpses of behavioral science, e.g., on new desired behaviors in the Change Impact Analysis or in the Transformation Dashboard, but certainly a more end-to-end deployment could create even more impact in specific initiatives.

When it comes to all, it is about the people side of the equation. It is easy to change strategy, process, or technology, but it is harder to change individuals, people, and their behaviors. I hope this book has provided some inspiration on how to bring the people side of change into play in an effective and impactful way.

INDEX

Note: Page numbers in italic refer to figures.

Printed in the United States
by Baker & Taylor Publisher Services